CW00566420

IMAGES
of Wales

LLANTRISANT

To keith

Very best wishes

Dean Powell

Sept '02

Llantrisant's most famous resident, Dr William Price (1800-1893), surgeon, Chartist, self-confessed Archdruid of Wales and prime-mover to legalize cremation in the British Isles. His obituary read: 'Dr William Price was certainly a figure of high romance. It was as though a composite creature had stepped out of the pages of Old Testament history and, in his passage through the centuries, had enriched his personality from the flow of all the hidden streams of myth and legend.'

IMAGES
of Wales

LLANTRISANT

Dean Powell

TEMPUS

Llantrisant-born author Dean Powell is a Freeman of the town and was recently elected a Trustee at the age of twenty-nine. A graduate of the University of Wales College of Swansea where he obtained a Bachelor of Arts degree in English and Welsh, Dean is the editor of the *Pontypridd & Llantrisant Observer* and literary editor of the *Western Mail*. A member of Treorchy Male Choir for almost fourteen years, he has undertaken a series of successful tours to Australia, Canada and America as their tenor soloist. He performs regularly in venues throughout the United Kingdom, has appeared on numerous commercial recordings and is frequently interviewed on radio and television. This is his third book for Tempus.

Dedication

This book is dedicated to the memory of my grandparents, Gwyneth (1911-1996) and Arthur Hooper (1910-1974). It is also written with thanks to my parents, Carole and David, not only for their love and support, but for making Llantrisant my home.

First published 2002
Copyright © Dean Powell, 2002

Tempus Publishing Limited
The Mill, Brimscombe Port,
Stroud, Gloucestershire, GL5 2QG
www.tempus-publishing.com

ISBN 0 7524 2497 1

TYPESETTING AND ORIGINATION BY
Tempus Publishing Limited
PRINTED IN GREAT BRITAIN BY
Midway Colour Print, Wiltshire

Contents

Introduction

'Dinas a osodir ar fryn ni ellir ei chuddio'
(*A City Set on a Hill Cannot Be Hid*)
Llantrisant Town Trust motto

Commanding an outstanding setting on the crest of a hill and enjoying the most picturesque viewpoint, Llantrisants splendour lies in its enchanting beauty and celebrated past. The glory of what was once a magnificent hilltop fortress town was crowned by its medieval castle and a fine parish church surrounded by a cluster of homes scattered throughout its charming, unplanned cobbled streets. Llantrisant became one of the most strategically important Norman strongholds in South Wales and as such has witnessed a colourful history of which its people remain justifiably proud.

Today, many of its landmark buildings stand as a testimony to a turbulent past, boasting a history of fierce battles, ancient customs and notorious characters, the likes of which we may never see again. Proud, quarrelsome and stubborn folk, members of large, feuding families have occupied these buildings for generations in a town where also resided Archdruids and eccentrics, lord mayors and Chartist leaders, murderers and captured kings of England. To explore fully such an extraordinary tale would take volumes to relate, but this mere glimpse gives a flavour of how Llantrisant developed into the thriving community it remains today.

Chiefly remarkable for its vantage point, it would not be unreasonable to believe that a Celtic community existed here at least as early as the seventh century and possibly as far back as the Roman invasion itself given the legion's interest in neighbouring lands. That settlement of largely timber dwellings within a wooden fort-like enclosure was probably a highly sophisticated, well organized post-Roman society, eventually overthrown by the conquering Norman barons centuries later. Pure speculation is the popular belief that the original settlement was called Llangawrdaf, probably fabricated by the likes of Iolo Morgannwg during his splendid re-writing of Welsh history during the eighteenth century.

Situated in the ancient Lordship of Meisgyn and Glynrhondda, early Christian ceremonies undoubtedly took place here following centuries of pagan worship. With the advent of Christianity, this extensive ecclesiastical centre, dedicated by missionaries of Llantwit Major to saints Illtyd, Gwynno and Dyfodwg, gave the town its present name of Church of the Three Saints. A Romanesque-styled church was probably built as early as 1096 by the first Norman lords who occupied the town and it was later rebuilt sometime around 1246 when the neighbouring castle was also fortified.

It was these Norman lords who recognized the advantages of further developing Llantrisant as a military base, owing to its elevation between the conquered vale and the barren mountain terrain of the north. In this hill country, or blaenau, the Celtic, or Welsh warriors gathered periodically to raid settlements from the invading Norman armies. Llantrisant was certainly ruled under Norman occupation by the early part of the twelfth century, becoming established as a fortress town under the leadership of Robert Consul, Earl of Gloucester, although he can hardly be congratulated for recognizing the site's potential. Gwrgan ab Ithel or Einon ab Collwyn, both Welsh lords of Glamorgan, may have built the first wooden fort, well before the Norman invasion.

Quite possibly, the first Norman castle was completed on this same site sometime between 1096 and 1100, its ringwork walls offering protection for a thriving community of smallholdings accompanied by the parish church. It was within such a settlement that those early Norman masters faced fierce opposition from the Celtic tribesmen and were probably expelled from

6

Llantrisant in one of many battles before 1127. Following their inevitable re-emergence, a stone-built defence of several towers, two wards and a timber ringwork with ditches were built by Gilbert de Clare in 1246, making it second only to Cardiff in military importance. In 1252 a daughter was born to the Earl of Gloucester, Richard de Clare at the castle and his eldest son, Gilbert the Red inherited it by 1262 while he built neighbouring Caerphilly. For the next two centuries the town, increasing to somewhere in the region of 190 houses by 1260, witnessed a series of bloodthirsty rebellions.

The most notable of which was the rebellion of Llewellyn Bren in 1316 which devastated the entire lordship, including Llantrisant, in just nine weeks. The castle, however, remained active until at least a decade later when it was used as an overnight prison for King Edward II, who was captured in November 1326 and later subjected to a horrifying execution at Berkeley Castle. Following a relatively short and chequered history as a fighting castle it was of little account from 1404 and it remains uncertain whether it was demolished at the hands of Owain Glyndwr during his raids against the English or possibly fell redundant when a period of greater stability emerged.

One of the most notable episodes in Llantrisant's history took place in 1346 with the presentation of its first known Charter, although historians have argued that such a document was entrusted to the people four centuries earlier. Tales of courageous longbowmen from the town fighting at the Battle of Crecy under Lord of Glamorgan Hugh Despenser, resulted in academics believing that was the reason behind those brave soldiers being rewarded with the issue of such a significant document. Sadly, the legend isn't so, because the Charter was actually presented five months earlier on 4 March 1346. However, it is always comforting to imagine that those gallant veterans of Crecy may have been the first to be bestowed with the freedom of the new Ancient Borough of Llantrisant on their return from victory.

The Charter was re-issued in 1424 and gave those Burgesses, or Freemen, absolute possession of the land, the equivalent of the freehold tenure we have today, and made it clear that non-Burgesses could not trade in the town without paying for the privilege. Therefore, a free borough, or corporation town, was a community of Freemen and its main purpose was to earn a corporate living. In an effort to help it to succeed in a competitive world its Burgesses gathered a range of privileges giving them a measure of self government, their own courts of law and control on markets and fairs. The portreeve exercised power over the administration while the corporation business itself was conducted by the Court Leet.

The boundary of the ancient borough was also sanctified by the custom of a religious ceremony, originated in the ninth century, which we now know as the Beating of the Bounds, and first recorded in Llantrisant in 1555. The eventual dissolution of the borough as a corporate town centuries later brought into being the Town Trust in 1889, to manage the Common, or Cymdda Fawr and Bach and Y Graig, Toll House and the Town Pumps, while admitting new hereditary Freemen on an annual basis.

Within a century of being issued its charter, Llantrisant of the late fourteenth and fifteenth century would hardly have been recognised by the inhabitants of a few generations before. Shortly after the Black Death swept through the Vale came Owain Glyndwr's wars when many of the English were dislodged and the Welsh moved to better lands. By 1514 Llantrisant declined to a village of no more than thirty white-washed homes and few immediate improvements were made during a period of comparative calm. The parish church underwent a process of rebuilding and by 1490 the west end was added along with a tower while the castle, however, was certainly ruined by the time Henry VIII's antiquarian, Leland, visited the town in 1536.

Llantrisant also held a somewhat dubious reputation as the haven of paupers, thieves and prostitutes and was a victim of drunkenness and rowdiness while outbreaks of epidemics were also widespread. The historic church vestry meeting on 5 December, 1783 was called to consult in regard of establishing a workhouse for the poor. Until then, the aged, feeble and weak-minded were either cared for by a neighbour for a small fee or simply left unassisted in insanitary cottages. In 1784 it was unanimously resolved to open the workhouse, the first in Glamorgan, in a series of adapted cottages along Swan Street and in the Black Cock Inn on Yr Allt, with the Union Workhouse opening a century later close to the Bull Ring.

Eventually the town reoccupied the high stance enjoyed during the medieval period and by the Victorian era witnessed a time of splendid refurbishment of the church and the appearance of many landmark houses, shops and inns which still exist today. Fairs and markets played a central role in its resurrection and the town's reputation as a centre for trade flourished. Four fairs were held annually in the open square adjoining the town hall and the Market House. The old town scales and weights were kept at the Angel Inn, or the Pwysty, where tolls were collected by the Constable of the Castle and imposed on goods entering the town for sale.

However, its certain degree of affluence as a hub of commercial activity, was relatively short-lived and gradually its authority declined in favour of neighbouring Newbridge. By the late eighteenth century a flourishing market was already in place there and the town, later renamed Pontypridd, enjoyed the facilities of the Glamorganshire Canal and Taff Vale Railway, none of which benefited Llantrisant in its seemingly awkward placement on a hill. Although Llantrisant railway station was opened in 1861, it was in thriving Pontyclun, three miles away. Ironically, Llantrisant's positioning, once its greatest attraction, was now something of a hindrance and although Lord Bute gave freedom for the market tolls it was not enough to save the town's commercial wealth.

However, the Victorian era still testifies to something of a golden age for Llantrisant when more than thirty well-established inns were open for business along with an astonishing forty shops in just a handful of streets. Population increased with the emergence of predominantly Cornish miners flocking to the mines at Mwyndy, along with immigrants who took up work on the neighbouring railway industry and tinplate works. Non-conformism played an active role in the social development of its people, with emphasis on sports, education, music and culture. A succession of chapels were built with startling frequency and thrived for generations while Welsh remained the predominant language of the inhabitants well into the early twentieth century.

The parish church, restored in 1873, played an active role in educating the people with no one more committed than Revd Powell Jones. This pioneer of modern education method, saw the building of the town's National School and showed desperate concern for the spiritual welfare of a population who 'played ball on Sunday' and 'could easily fall victim to atheism'. It was hardly an unfounded threat either, particularly when considering the influence exerted by the local surgeon, Dr William Price, Llantrisant's most colourful character, whose spectacular eccentricities totally outshone the town's celebrated son, David Evans, and his ascendancy to becoming the Lord Mayor of London.

For more than a thousand years this town has witnessed a truly fascinating history of rebellions and customs, characters and events that has captured the imagination of every fortunate visitor. For its sons and daughters, Llantrisant's alluring charm can be understood by walking the very streets where these episodes occurred. Quite simply, we are proud to call this unique hilltop town our home.

Dean Powell
Tŷ Ffynnon
Newbridge Road
Llantrisant
May 2002

One
People and Places

Cefn y Mabley Farm, c. 1905. Pictured from left to right: Thomas 'The Butch' Davies (1877-1960), Margaret Davies (1877-1966) with baby Blodwyn, later Westcott, (1904-1989), Edward Arthur Rees (1833-1913), Mary Jamunia Rees (1871-1936) who later married Jacob John, bachelor William Rees (1874-1951) and the little girl is Gladys Rees. Edward Rees, a collier, became a Freeman in May 1871 through his wife, Mary Davies (1833-1895).

Llantrisant from New Parc Farm, c. 1900. Our journey through the town begins with a view of what was once a fortress of immense military importance. Probably dating from the seventh century, those early Celtic settlers provided the basis for a highly-sophisticated society, later conquered by the Norman lords and the site of countless battles. It was once described by a visiting missionary as the only place in Britain to resemble the city of Jerusalem.

Llantrisant, c. 1910. During the eighteenth century the town had a reputation as being unhealthy and prone to frequent outbreaks of serious epidemics. In 1764 the diarist William Thomas blamed the death of forty residents in less than fourteen days on the vapours emitting from the nearby coal mine.

Llantrisant, c. 1920. Following Talbot Road towards Southgate, notice Parc View Cottage close to the centre, once a surgery used by Dr Willy Davies. Next to the Wesleyan chapel is a row of three-storey houses with the Southgate Turnpike Toll House on the extreme right. It was demolished during the mid-1920s.

Southgate, c. 1905. Southgate Cottage was built in 1785 and during the first half of the twentieth century was home to the Phillips family who later moved into No. 1 High Street on the opposite side of the bend. When this photograph was taken, the shop adjoining the cottage, which later became James' Grocers and Dairy, was being built.

Southgate, *c.* 1940. By the time this photograph was taken the Turnpike Toll House had been demolished, but along the lower part of Southgate bend stood a row of three homes occupied by the Phillips, Evans and Baker families. The houses were demolished during the mid-1960s.

Tŷ Plocyn pictured from the Southgate bend, *c.* 1940. Originally a farmhouse, it later became a butchers shop for Morgan the Plocyn and, since it was situated opposite Dr J.C.R. Morgans surgery in Southgate House, part of the property became a pharmacists run by Marcus Rees. One of the towns first doctors was Watkin Evans in 1780, listed as 'surgeon and apothecary and charged to attend the poor and supply them with plaster and medicines.'

Dr John Clifford Rowland Morgan (1895-1964). Born in Llanwynno in August 1895 he was educated at Mill Hill School and Cardiff Medical School. He experienced active service during the First World War in Egypt and Palestine and resumed training at Westminster Hospital before qualifying in 1921. Dr Jack followed Dr Willy Davies as the Llantrisant General Practitioner. Married to Dr Sybil Magnola Rees (born 1898), in 1922 he built Southgate House (on the site of a cottage, dated 1865) and opened a surgery in the basement, with his sister Gladys as the receptionist. An authority on Bach, Dr Jack formed the Llantrisant and District Choral Society in 1931 and enjoyed considerable success as its conductor, the highlight being a performance of 'The Dream of Gerontius' at the Three Valleys Festival in 1939. He retired to Penarth in 1953 and died at Llandough Hospital, aged sixty-nine.

Southgate and the start of High Street, c. 1955. Pictured on the doorstep are Ellen Phillips (wife of Alfred) and her daughter Yvonne (later wife to Gordon Miles). In the grocery shop opposite, the proprietor Harry James (whose brother Walter owned Gwalia Stores), started a dairy business which was later taken over by Mervyn Collins.

High Street, *c*. 1915. The entrance on the right leads to Llantrisant Cottage and the high roof of Elim Trinity (Presbyterian) chapel, which opened in 1876, can be seen in the background.

Llantrisant Cottage, built in the mid-nineteenth century, *c*. 1909. In the 1920s it was used as a working men's club with its own snooker hall before Charlie Riddle bought the property along with Llantrisant House and the nearby cottages. During the 1930s and 40s part of the cottage became a surgery for dentist Mr Morgan.

Tŷ'r Clettwr, with Penelopen and Nicholas Price standing outside, 1894. As the home of Dr William Price it enjoyed a colourful history. When he cremated his infant child, Iesu Grist on 13 January 1884, the house came under attack from a hostile mob while the baby's grieving mother, Gwenllian Llewellyn remained alone inside. Tŷ'r Clettwr was later demolished and replaced by Zoar (Soar) chapel in 1902.

Rose Hill, High Street, c. 1910. In later years Marshall Sparnon owned a shop on the hill, with Watkin Davies running a cobblers business on the opposite side. Further along, on the left was Crown Stores, one of the oldest businesses in the town and later run by Collwyn Davies.

High Street, *c.* 1910. Bradford House (left) was a fine drapery shop, owned by Miss Silkstone. Next door is Penuel chapel, which opened in 1826. Typically, the chapel stood opposite a public house, called the Fox & Hounds with the Wheatsheaf Hotel and Horse & Groom taverns in close proximity.

The junction of High Street leading left and Commercial Street straight ahead towards Newbridge Road, *c.* 1910. Some of the businesses that operated at this time included Mrs Peters' Drapery, Kennedy Milk, Mrs Parker's Shoe Repairs, a chemist, barber and a library. On the right is Llantrisant post office, home to a telephone exchange by 1928. A dubious operation since it was noted that telephone conversations could not be held in private, allowing the office to become the starting point for local gossip!

Llantrisant from East Caerlan in 1898. The Court Leet of Freemen called on Lady Windsor, the lady of the manor for financial support to rebuild the town hall and Cornmarket in 1773, which resulted in the increase of tolls on entering the town on market day and a clear government for regulating the market was imposed. In 1779 Llywelyn John and Rees John became overseers, but documents reveal that competency was hardly their strong point, with one typical entry reading: 'Very remiss in their duty in not weighing bread and butter upon market days which belongs to their duty to do'.

Llantrisant from East Caerlan, c. 1940. The old town has been home to a plethora of unique individuals, such as Hopkin Hopkins, allegedly the world's smallest man. The second son of dwarf Lewis Hopkins, he was baptized on 29 January 1736 and spent most of his life exhibited in carnivals throughout the country. Originally from Caercyrlais near Tonyrefail, the young man suffered from Progeria, a childhood disorder characterized by dwarfism and premature senility. At the time of his death in 1754, aged 18, he weighed just 13lbs and was 2ft 7ins tall.

Elizabeth O'Connor of Heol y Graig, October 1937 shortly before her death. The elderly Bessie O'Connor was pictured in Talbot Green, awaiting the visit of the Duke of Kent while wearing a collection of war medals awarded to her brother who lost his life during the First World War. Unknowingly, she had pinned the Union Jack on her coat upside-down. Miss O'Connor owned a small shop below Tabor Baptist chapel on High Street where she made tea and cakes. In later years she moved to Heol y Graig to be close to her surviving brother, Jack, who worked in the Cwm (colliery). A staunch Catholic, she walked the ten-mile round trip to church services in Treforest, every Sunday.

Llantrisant pictured from Erw Hir, c. 1925. Better known as Long Acre, or The Acre, this path led to a quarry from which the majority of the stone was taken to build many of the houses in the town during the growth in prosperity of the nineteenth century. The first property built on this stretch of track was Erw Hir House in 1905.

Llantrisant Castle, c. 1900. A proud edifice during medieval times, it kept watch over the valleys to the north during a war-torn period. A stone-built defence, it may have been formed on an even earlier stronghold built by Celtic Lord Gwrgan ap Ithel. Occupied in the early twelfth century, prior to the Norman lords' first expulsion from the town during a series of Welsh revolutions, it was fortified in 1246 by Gilbert de Clare and second only to Cardiff in military importance.

Twr y Gigfran (Ravens Tower) and the town hall, c. 1900. In 1252 a daughter called Margaret was born to Earl of Gloucester Richard de Clare at the castle. His eldest son Gilbert the Red occupied it by 1262 and went on to build Caerphilly Castle. Raided by supporters of Llywelyn ap Gruffydd, it had a turbulent history as a fighting castle. Severely damaged in four Welsh attacks, it was destroyed in 1315 during Llewellyn Bren's revolution and was of little account from 1404, possibly demolished by Owain Glyndwr. The Marquis of Bute used its stonework to repair Cardiff and Caerphilly castles and build Castell Coch, while locals took the stones to build nearby homes.

Llantrisant Castle, 1910. On 16 November 1326, the castle, run by Constable Robert de Aston, was used as a prison for the captured King Edward II who was later brutally murdered at Berkeley Castle. The weak monarch had inherited constitutional troubles and when Queen Isabella, his wife, plotted against him, helped by her lover Roger Mortimer, disaster ensued when the King's supporters, the Despensers of Caerphilly took up arms against the Hereford Mortimers. The King fled to Neath Abbey, but failed to recruit an army. In November, he was guided by a Cistercian monk, (a Mortimer spy) for refreshment at Penrhys. Heading for the safety of Llantrisant where he proposed to spend the remainder of his life, Edward II was intercepted at Pant y Brad – the Hollow of Treason – in Tonyrefail and imprisoned in Llantrisant Castle.

View of the Graig from the castle. In August 1919 the Town Trust held a meeting to investigate why the Independent Labour Party were holding political meetings on the Graig every Sunday without prior permission from the Trust. A letter was sent to Idwal Williams of Swan Street, disallowing them access to the Graig until consent was granted.

William Morgan (1804-1869), Portreeve (or mayor) of Llantrisant in 1867. Known as Billy Caergwanaf, he was a lively, powerfully built son of farmer Thomas Morgan. He married Catherine Jones, of Monknash, on 18 August 1833 and had three children named Martha, Edward and Catherine. By 1841 they lived at Caergwanaf Farm near Miskin, and moved to Ty Isaf farm in 1851 before settling in the Ivor Arms, Brynsadler. On 21 February 1861 a brutal attack was made on W. Morgan, who was well known for his philanthropy and kindness to the inhabitants of this neighbourhood. It was revealed the perpetrator was the young ex-portreeve Josiah Lewis. In April a private adjournment took place, the cross summonses were dismissed and each party was ordered to pay costs. On 17 June 1869 Morgan died of bronchitis at the Ivor Arms.

(John) Taliesin Morgan (1849-1922). Born in the White Hart pub on the Bull Ring on 21 November 1849, he was the son of David and Eleanor Morgan. His grandfather was David Jones who, aged seventy, had tenancy of the pub in 1842 from R. Rickards. Taliesin's other grandfather, Richard Morgan, owned the tailor's shop on the Bull Ring. Taliesin, who also became a tailor, was inaugurated as a Freeman on 26 May 1871 and became the clerk of the newly formed Llantrisant Town Trust from March 1891 to October 1904. Probably his greatest contribution was publishing the second *History of Llantrisant* in 1898 (following Sem Phillips's volume in 1866). He died in Cardiff on 19 August 1922.

Y Felin Wynt, the thirteenth-century tower, is unlikely to have been the windmill believed to have been destroyed in one of many battles between the Normans and the Welsh prior to 1280. Enjoying such a high vantage point it was probably an auxillary tower to the castle, and was certainly used as such in Napoleonic times. The circular stone tower, known locally as the Billy Wynt, was restored as a folly in 1890 at the request of the Town Trust. The surveyor, Gomer Morgan was paid £15.

Church Street pictured from the Graig. On the left of the picture, directly below the church wall, stood a row of five terraced cottages called South Parade. When the church wall collapsed during the 1930s many of the homes, occupied by the Dooley and Lock families, were damaged and later demolished.

John Powell John (1885-1950). Known as Pow John, he was the son of Thomas John of West Caerlan Farm. Christened the 'Mayor of Llantrisant' by fellow farmers, he was a cattle dealer and agent for the Bute estate. With an interest in the Farmers Union and the local fox-hunting group, he was also a member of Llantrisant Town Trust. He married Mary Hannah Richards (1897-1979) of Tyr Pantyscawen Farm and they had three children named Anne, Mary and David. In 1948 West Caerlan, the eighteenth-century farmhouse, burned down, forcing the family to move to Maes yr Haul in Cross Inn. On 26 December 1950 he was walking near this farm when he was struck down by a car. He died three days later, aged sixty-five.

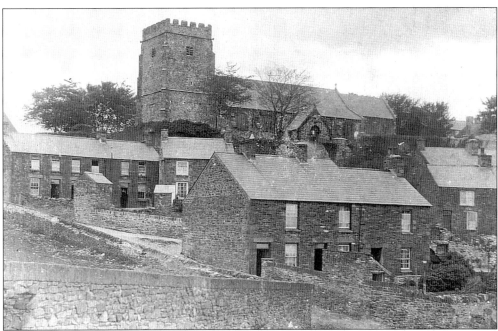

Llantrisant parish church and Church Street. According to legend, although probably a suspect tale originated from the likes of Iolo Morgannwg, who was prone to elaborate on Welsh history, a spot near the church was called the Tomb of Bronwen. It is said to have derived from a tradition that a Queen of Ireland died there following a blow to the head caused by her husband.

Tudor John (1908-2001). Born in the Pwysty, he was the son of stonemason William (1874-1956) and Amy John and was brought up in Dan y Castell house. Educated at Pontypridd Grammar School he studied chemistry at the University of Wales, Cardiff and graduated with an MSc before joining the navy. A severe illness brought the young sailor home and eventually he joined his father as a stonemason, becoming responsible for building many of the modern properties along Church Street. An elected member of Llantrisant and District Rural Council he remained firmly based in the town where he raised his five children. He served on Taff Ely Borough Council as a local representative and later Mid Glamorgan County Council.

William Clanford Beavan (1894-1968) of Church Street. Better known as Glan, he served on the HMS *Vivid* during the First World War and later spent most of his life working in the nearby iron ore. He was better known as a cobbler who worked in a shed at the back of his home. His wife, Theresa Richards (1894-1976) was brought up on Tyr Pantyscawen Farm, Heol Las, and her sister, Mary Hannah Richards married Pow John of West Caerlan Farm.

Ernie Jenkins driving the council's steam roller towards Heol y Graig, *c.* 1925. Mr Jenkins, who later married Nelly Morris, lived in Heol y Beiliau (The Pitching), where this photograph was taken. For many years he worked for the Llantrisant and District Rural Council, repairing roads in the area.

Heol y Beiliau, better known as The Pitching, which led from Heol y Graig to the turning on to Greyhound Lane and Heol Sticil y Beddau, also led into Sunnybank and Ceridwen Terrace. The cottage on the furthest end of Sunnybank was demolished in the late 1950s. The house in the middle of the pitching was once home to Lila Dyer, while Ty-yn-y-Berllan house can be seen on the right.

Leo Ward (1923-1982) pictured in Durban, 1940. Born in Sunnybank, Leo was serving in the Royal Artillery during the Second World War when he was captured by the Japanese while fighting in the Far East. For the next four years he survived the horrors of a prisoner of war camp in Sumatra along with gruelling work on the Burma Railway and the bridge over the Kwai river. Months went by before his parents were informed that the teenager had been taken captive, and not been killed as originally believed. He later worked as a conductor on Rhondda transport although ill health, due to the war years, plagued him for the rest of his life. He married Margaret Hughes of Treherbert and the couple settled in Dan Caerlan where they raised a son, Terrance.

Greyhound Lane leading towards Heol-Sticil-y-Beddau, originally called Ystycyl y Beddau on the 1871 Ordnance Survey map. A nineteenth-century historian wrote: 'Llantrisant's narrow streets, disregard of rules of architecture, adds much to its beauty.'

The Elizabethan House on High Street, later renamed Yr Allt. The wooden structure was demolished during the 1950s when a wagon travelling down the cobbled lane towards Church Street struck the building and made it unsafe. The site later became a timber yard for builder Tudor John.

Yr Allt (little hill) taken from Church Street. Originally known as High Street (and called by this name well into the twentieth century while the other High Street existed), Yr Allt ran north to south through the centre of a medieval walled settlement with the church and castle on either side. This was probably the oldest street in the town and eventually joined Swan Street which runs east to west.

To the Right Honourable
David Evans
Lord Mayor of London

We, the undersigned, on behalf of the Inhabitants of your Native Town of Llantrisant, desire to tender your Lordship this expression of our warmest congratulations upon your attainment of the highest Civil Office in the greatest City in the World.

We cannot but feel that this happy event sheds honour, both upon the Principality of Wales and upon the little Welsh Town which boasts of the unique privilege of having a Lord Mayor of London as one of its Burgesses, and a valued member of its Town Trust. We feel that this close connection with one who holds your Lordship's high position of dignity, at the very centre of the Commerce & Civilization of the World, ought to have a most beneficial and elevating influence upon all the Inhabitants of the Town and Parish of Llantrisant. For it will make us feel that we belong to, and have an interest in, that greater world in the centre of which one of ourselves, as it were, now holds the most conspicuous place.

We shall watch with a new interest, during the coming year, the various great events and movements of National and, it may be, of Imperial importance, with which your name will be associated. And we pray that you may be given strength and wisdom from above, to enable you to discharge with credit to yourself, with honour to your native land, and with advantage to the great City over whose destinies you have been called for a season to preside, the important duties of your high position. Signed on behalf of the subscribers:

CHAIRMAN Evan John.   VICE-CHAIRMAN J. Whiteland Hughes

Roderick Lewis   William Williams

Taliesin Morgan HON. SECRETARY

November 9th 1891.

A congratulatory address presented to David Evans, Lord Mayor of London, by the people of Llantrisant. It was later returned to the Town Trust in 1945 from its owner, Mr Green of Kent, for the sum of £3. Born on 21 April 1849 at Glanmuchydd Farm, David Evans was the son of farmer and maltster Thomas Evans. After attending the local school he went to a seminary at Merton, Surrey. In 1866 his uncle, Richard Evans, head of a firm of merchants at Watling Street, London, appointed him as a partner. On completing his education in France, he became a Freeman in 1870 and later married Emily Boakes, finally settling into a mansion in Ewell Grove with their eight children. In 1875 he was approached by friends in the ward of Corwainer, City of London, to become a candidate for the seat in the Court of Common Council.

28

Sir David Evans KCMG, Lord Mayor of London (1849-1907), at the Welsh National Presentation Testimonial Fund, Mansion House, 1892. Elected Alderman of the Borough of Llantrisant in 1883, and Alderman of the City of London for the ward of Castle Baynard, in 1885 he was made Sheriff of London and Middlesex, and in 1891 became Lord Mayor of London. He made a state visit to Cardiff in July 1892 and travelled to Llantrisant to open a bazaar, which raised £400 in aid of Llantrisant church restoration fund. The procession in an open-top carriage, led by the town band, took him through the streets. On 30 July 1892 under Her Majesty Queen Victoria's direction, he was made a Knight Commander of the Most Distinguished Order of St Michael and St George. He died in August 1907, aged fifty-eight.

Will Wild (1858-1934), the drover of Heol Las c. 1920. Four times a year, gypsies would visit Llantrisant Fair and it was his job to take the tethered horses to Commercial Street and trot them along the road to examine their level of fitness. He also worked as a farmhand, digging ditches and cutting hedges in return for a hearty meal. A well-known character of the town, he was certainly no stranger to the local public houses. He was buried in Llantrisant churchyard on 11 December 1934, aged seventy-six.

Aerial view of Llantrisant, 1967. With a little imagination, the reader can see the ancient boundaries of the early fortified town. Set on the top of the hill, the picture shows the oval-shaped enclosure that probably surrounded the church and the castle with a few houses within

the main castle walls. The street running through the very centre of the original fortress is Yr Allt, once appropriately called High Street.

Heol Las (Blue Street), 1902. Pictured on the right is Tyr Pantyscawen Farmhouse, built in 1874 on a site where an earlier farm probably existed. Some believe it was used as a vicarage since many of the steps leading to the old cowshed were tombstones. Covering an area of 8.7 acres, it was originally owned by the Richards family and later transferred to John Powell John, whose wife was born there. In 1950 it was bought by Bronwen and William Roberts who were forced to sell the land under compulsory purchase for £750 to make way for the Common Housing Estate.

Heol Las c. 1920. One of the dwellings on the right is Vicarage Cottage, which is followed by the turning on to the long drive that led to Llantrisant vicarage. On the opposite side of the road stood one of several pumps in the town.

Llantrisant from the Malt House fields. Prior to a major smallpox epidemic during the 1890s, a row of cottages existed at the rear of Swan Street. It was named Glyn Terrace since the occupants were mostly miners who worked in the Glyn Colliery. When many of the families, probably Cornish settlers, succumbed to the disease, the houses were set alight in an effort to rid the town of smallpox. Some of the family graves are inscribed 'Not To Be Opened'.

The Malt House (Bracdy). A two-winged building, with the second section built in 1830 by the Evans family, the earliest-known maltster was Hopkins who worked there in 1750. Succeeded by William Evans, better known as Wil Bragwr, who was a maltster until 1870, it was later owned by John Davies and turned into a farm. It had 60 acres, with eight large fields and one of them, Cae Shams (James' Field), was where, in the late Victorian era, Methodist revival meetings were held. The family enjoyed international renown as the producers of award-winning cheeses between 1880 and 1930.

Heol y Sarn, (Common Road), was once home to a blacksmith's shop situated next to the Bear Inn, occupied in 1841 by Thomas Evans. Shoemaker James Morgan, or Siamsy Crydd also lived close by. One day he was witnessing the bull-baiting on the Bull Ring when he caught a white terrier in his leather apron as it was tossed in the air by one of the bulls. The bull charged in the direction of Morgan's pregnant wife, Jennet, who was so terrified by the beast she died in premature labour.

Heol y Sarn. On the right is Cae Ysgubor Farm, a property once owned by Dr William Price and later home to the Alexander family. To the left can be seen the white chimney-top of the Welcome to Town public house, demolished during the late 1940s to make way for the Common Housing Estate. A dairy also existed opposite the Butcher's Arms.

Common Road with Llantrisant in the background. In 1868 a great commotion was caused amongst the Freemen when the Lord of the Manor, the Marquis of Bute, consented for T. Powell Esq to search for coal under the common lands. The Freemen felt they had rights to it. Operations began and the Trustees rose up in arms. But the manorial rights of the town and the minerals had been purchased by Sir William Herbert from Edward VI in 1551, later under the ownership of Lord Bute. Operations continued but were later abandoned.

The Common duck pond, which existed from 1822 onwards. The original town pond was situated within the boundaries of the castle. In July 1924, sanitary inspector Richard Grabham declared the Common pond should be cleaned or filled in because it had become a cesspit. A few years later many of the Freemen, opposed to golf being played on the Common, threw flags, balls and discs from the course into the pond in protest. Until 1946 a popular dance pavilion also occupied the land to the rear.

Margaret Davies (1877-1966), the author's great-grandmother, pictured outside her home, No. 11 Newbridge Road. She was one of eight children born to Edward Rees and Mary Davies of Cefn Mabley Farm. In September 1898 she married Thomas Albert Davies of Nantymoel, better known as Tom 'Butch', and the couple had two daughters, Blodwyn (later Westcott) and Gwyneth (later Hooper) and two sons who died in infancy. The three-storey house, situated at the top of Gwaun Ruperra, was demolished in the late 1950s when it was deemed structurally unsafe and the elderly couple moved to St David's Place.

The Common Estate being built in the early 1950s on land taken under a compulsory purchase order from Tyr Pantyscawen Farm. Its street names were adopted from the three patron saints of the parish church: Illtyd, Gwynno and Dyfodwg.

Newbridge Road c. 1910. The terraced street along the road which led towards Newbridge (later Pontypridd) was built from 1867 onwards, although a series of ancient wells, probably dating from 1750, may prove that dwellings existed there much earlier than that date. It was also home to several public houses, including the Castle Inn (once owned by Mary Jones), Thomas Edwards's brewery in adjoining St David's Place and, further along, the Brynteg Arms.

Dan Caerlan council housing estate, June 1951. This picture was taken from the bedroom window of No. 43 and shows the massive array of decorations to commemorate the Festival of Britain. A close-knit housing estate of seventy-eight pre-fabricated homes built following the Second World War, it was home to a number of large families, including ones by the name of Hurley, Rees, Jenkins, Bryant and Dobbins.

Left: Trevor Evans. Born in 1933 on Yr Allt to Charles and Eiddwen Evans (formerly John), he later moved to Dan Caerlan. On 7 February 1952 he joined the Welsh Regiment and Private 22636212 Evans found himself on a six-week boat trip to Hong Kong to serve in the Forgotten War of Korea. His regiment was dispatched to South Korea and on 28 May the Chinese launched a vicious attack that lasted four hours and would become one of the last major conflicts of the war – Hook Hill. A shell exploded near Private Evans, killing two friends and injuring his legs, later causing gangrene. Missing in action and believed dead, the town celebrated when the news arrived on 31 August that he was alive, and following surgery by a French Canadian medical team, his legs were saved.

Below: Norman, Lorna, Dorothy (Dolly) and Margaret Evans with Glynne Holmes, 1948. They are facing the new development of Dan Caerlan with the lower end of Newbridge Road and the entrance to Bull Ring Farm behind them. Contrary to popular belief this area of Llantrisant, known as Davidstown, is unlikely to have been named followed the ascent of local boy David Evans to Lord Mayor of London. Mysteriously enough, decades before that a field on the south of Newbridge Road was called Cae Dafydd (David's Field).

Gwyneth Morgan, Bull Ring Farm (1914-1999) pictured in 1937. The first child of farmer William Morgan, she was better known as Gwyneth Siams. A local celebrity due to her beautiful singing voice, she was often heard throughout the town while milking the cows during the early mornings. After receiving some formal vocal training, she became a much-sought-after soloist, accompanied by pianist Lottie Williams. During the Second World War they often performed for the injured troops being treated at Miskin Manor. Gwyneth later married Edward Cornelius and continued singing in public well into her later years. Her younger sister is Mary Morgan (later Williams).

William Morgan, Bull Ring Farm (1885-1934) c. 1910. Better known as Billy Siams, he married Anne Jayne Davies, niece to John Davies of the Malthouse and they had two daughters, Gwyneth (above) and Mary. His father, James Morgan, bought Bull Ring Farm in 1868 and became a Trustee of Llantrisant in July 1903. A well-known haulier, he would fetch coal from the railway station at Cross Inn and supply homes around the town. James Morgan, known by his Welsh name, Siams Morgan, died in March 1905.

Dr William Price (1800-1893). Born in Rudry, the fifth child of Revd William Price, he was an apprentice to surgeon Evan Edwards at the age of thirteen and later studied at St Bartholomew's Hospital, London, where he was made a Licentiate of the Society of Apothecaries and a Member of the Royal College of Surgeons before turning twenty-two. In 1827 he moved to Nantgarw and became the surgeon for ironmaster Francis Crawshay, practising medicine at the Brown Lenox chainworks. Claiming to be an Archdruid he carried out ancient rites at the Rocking Stone. The local clergy tried to convince the press he had desecrated his father's grave and cut off his head something Price admitted in an effort to prove his father was insane when signing his will.

Dr William Price, Gwenllian, Penelopen and Nicholas c. 1892. A leader of the failed Chartist rising, he fled to France disguised as a woman, where he claimed to have become a friend of the brother-in-law of King Louis Philippe. In 1860 he built the Round Houses at Glyntaf as an entrance to a planned stately home which failed. In 1873 he was acquitted of the manslaughter of a patient and settled in Llantrisant, joined by his housekeeper, Gwenllian Llewellyn who gave birth to their first child, Iesu Grist (Jesus Christ) in August 1883. The infant died on 10 January 1884 and he cremated it in a container of paraffin oil on East Caerlan. This act of blasphemy caused a riot in the town, and the corpse was dragged from the flames, but Price succeeded in cremating it on 21 March.

Cremation programme to Dr William Price, 1893. In March 1884, he conducted his own defence brilliantly at the Crown Court trial over his son's cremation, a typical showman who played to the crowded gallery, claiming, 'It is not right that a carcass should be allowed to rot and decompose in this way. It results in a wastage of good land, pollution of the earth, water and air, and is a constant danger to all living creatures'. He was acquitted by Justice Stephens, paving the way for the passing of the Cremation Act of 1902. He was bold enough to challenge existing beliefs and defy convention, question the justice system, poured scorn on orthodox religion, despised the law and belittled medical theories.

Gwenllian Llewellyn (1859-c. 1933). Originally from Pontypridd, she came to Llantrisant as Dr Price's housekeeper in 1875, aged sixteen. Seven years later she gave birth to their first child, Iesu Grist, who died within the month. Dr Price, by then in his eighties, also fathered two other children with Miss Llewellyn (whom he never married) called Penelopen and Iesu Grist the second (later renamed Nicholas). Following Dr Price's death they moved to the Butcher's Arms and she married John Parry of Llanharan who built East Caerlan House in 1906. The couple had a daughter, Rachel, who lived at the house for the remainder of her life.

The cremation of Dr William Price, Tuesday 31 January 1893. After a fall he took to his settee and died at 9 p.m. on Monday 23 January 1893. His last words were 'Give me champagne'. He had often been seen walking the mountains naked, reciting Welsh poetry, or parading through the town dressed in a white tunic, scarlet waistcoat, green trousers and fox-skin hat, carrying the Druidic symbols of a burning torch and crescent moon. His mind also fell prey to a form of schizophrenia, claiming that Homer was from Caerphilly, and confusing himself with a twelfth-century Welsh Prince.

Cremation of Dr William Price, 1893. Having already planned his cremation, the body was placed in an iron coffin made by the local blacksmith. At 8 a.m. on January 31 a ceremony was conducted by Revd Daniel Fisher, curator of Llantrisant, before a congregation of 20,000 people on the summit of East Caerlan. The cremation took eight hours, on a spot marked by a 60ft white pole surmounted by a crescent moon. A carnival mood prevailed, with the pubs running dry in the town.

Penelopen Price (1886-1977). Dr Price's only daughter, Penelopen was a gifted musician and scholar. Brought up at the Butcher's Arms, before moving to East Caerlan House, she became a qualified nurse and was recognized for her services to the Red Cross during World War I. Throughout her life, she was best known as the local piano teacher who would travel from home to home on horseback to give lessons. On 30 November 1953 she opened Thornhill Crematorium and in October 1966 she unveiled a stained-glass window in memory of her father at Glyntaff Crematorium where she was cremated in 1977, having died at the age of ninety-one.

Nicholas Price (1890-1956). A mysterious figure, Nicholas was originally named Iesu Grist (Jesus Christ) in memory of his dead brother who was cremated at East Caerlan. Briefly married, before fleeing the area to live in America for a lengthy period to avoid national conscription, Nicholas spent most of his life at East Caerlan where presumably he worked on the farm. He was also a carpenter and worked for builder Will John at the RAF aerodrome in St Athan before spending time in Newport. He was best remembered as a heavy drinker and bare-knuckle fighter in the streets of Llantrisant after dark. Although immaculately dressed, he adopted some of his fathers eccentricities by never wearing socks.

Penelopen Price unveiling a bronze plaque in memory of her father at Zoar chapel, the site of his former home, Tŷ'r Clettwr, on 17 September 1947. She was joined by the Lord Mayor of Cardiff, members of Llantrisant Town Trust, Councillor Ivor Jacob, Arthur Pearson, MP for Pontypridd, and Hugh Royle, the chairman of the Federation of British Cremation Authorities.

A crowd of more than 300 people turned out for the unveiling of Dr William Price's commemorative plaque (17 September 1947) in a town which had once persecuted him for his beliefs. Following the unveiling ceremony the crowd sang 'Cwm Rhondda' and the Welsh national anthem 'Hen Wlad Fy Nhadau'.

Two
Religion and Education

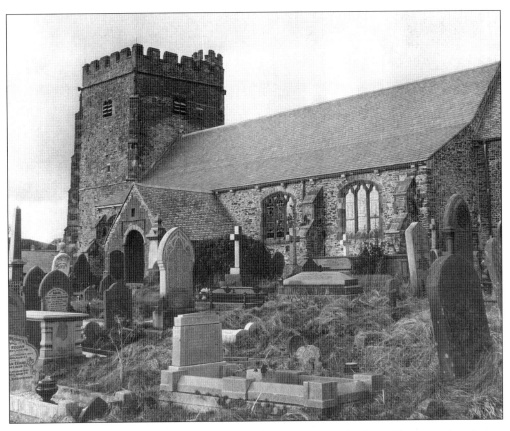

Llantrisant parish church pictured from the south in 1967. The first Christian church was probably built on a site once used for pagan worship. The village was converted by the monks of Illtyd from Llantwit Major who dedicated the church to their patron saints Illtyd, Gwynno and Dyfodwg, giving the town its name. All that is left of that first church is the Resurrection Stone, illustrating an ancient Celtic wheel cross, still kept in the building.

Aerial view of the church. The original Romanesque-style church was probably rebuilt on the site of a Celtic place of worship in 1096, although it underwent further rebuilding in 1246. Only the font and a section of the south door remain from the original building which became the mother church of a parish that extended to the Breconshire border. In 1386 it was under the jurisdiction of the Abbot of Tewkesbury until it was dissolved in 1539, then came under the Dean and Chapter of Gloucester who remained in charge until 1885 when the Bishop of Llandaff took over responsibility.

North view of the church c. 1920, showing the chimney connected to the vestry fireplace. The late middle ages was a time of splendid rebuilding of the church. The 70ft tower and west end were added around 1490, although indications show a medieval tower once stood on the same spot. In 1718 a peal of six bells were hung, each one inscribed.

Revd Evan Morgan (1787-1864). Morgan was the vicar of Llantrisant from 1845 until his death on 22 November 1864. Originally from Llanbadarn, West Wales, his wife, Letitia was from Buckinghamshire and the couple had three daughters, named Letitia, Amelia and Augusta. He was also a formidable Justice of the Peace for Glamorgan when the police court was held for many years at the Cross Keys Hotel on High Street. Colliery prosecutions and other contractual questions from the Rhondda were held in the same court during this time.

Canon J. Powell Jones BD (1833-1883). Born in Llysnony, Gorseinon, he was educated at Bowen's Academy, Swansea, where he distinguished himself as the best scholar. At seventeen he entered St David's College, Lampeter, and was appointed assistant tutor before his twenty-second birthday. Regarded as one of the rising hopes of the church in Wales, this refined, elegant, engaging, dignified and commanding man was vicar of Llantrisant from 1865 until his death in the vicarage on 21 December 1883. Canon Jones, who was made a Freeman in September 1865, was a pioneer of modern educational methods in South Wales, and during his tenure saw the National School built on West Caerlan in 1867.

Church interior prior to the 1873 refurbishment. The vestry was the meeting place for leading landowners of the parish and where common lands and roads were administered, cheese tithes decided upon and an overseer of the poor appointed. The parish register read: 'David Harry was allowed 6d weekly for taking care of Mary David being lunatic.' Parish records were allegedly burned in 1728, but many interesting entries were made by Revd Richard Harries. On 25 September 1751 he wrote: 'Evan Jenkins buried; last Saturday he was here, Sunday at Gelliwastad, Monday sickened, Tuesday died!!! O Adam!' On 26 December 1758 the vicar related: 'Mary Bowen sent for me to christen her daughter soon after her father attempted to kill me in my own house. If I had not been too strong for him, he would have killed me.'

Llantrisant parish church interior c. 1964, following the removal of the gas lamps on the arches. In 1873 the interior was rebuilt, costing £3,000 and influenced by architect John Pritchard, allowing a certain charm and beauty of a Victorian Gothic design. In 1894 the west end was completely restored, costing £1,200. The bells were rehung and a 4ft-deep white marble baptistry, for baptism by immersion, was placed under the floor of the choir vestry. A carved oak screen was installed in memory of Canon Powell Jones.

The east window, created by Morris Burne-Jones, was placed above the altar during the renovations of 1873. It is one of only two known stained-glass windows (the other is in Cologne Cathedral) depicting Christ without a beard. An effigy of a warrior was placed on the nearby wall, said to represent Cadwgan Fawr of Miskin who opposed Gilbert de Clare when the Norman lord attempted to suppress Welsh custom in the town.

The parish church and West Caerlan Farm pictured *c.* 1900. Prior to 1900 a cottage and garden existed below the tower, property of the same family that owned the Malthouse on Heol Las. A request was made by the clergy to extend the churchyard, and the owner of the Malthouse, John Davies, gave it to the church as a gift. Most of the Davies family are now buried there.

The vicarage from Heol Las *c.* 1930. The original vicarage was demolished in 1770 and a new one built under the guidance of Revd Robert Rickards in 1776. The vicar's family owned several properties in the town, including the Rickard's Arms on Swan Street (later the workingmen's club). The vicarage, also home to a large household staff, was demolished in 1965 while Revd Edwin Davies was vicar and a new house built nearby.

Llantrisant Tableaux 1916. From left to right, back row: M. Williams, F. Westcott, Lilla Dyer, E. Morgan, H. Richards, M. Davies, J. Traylor, E. Davies, David Lukey. Middle row: L.R. Davies, P. Hopkins, G. John, L. Cook, J. Williamson, M. Davies, B. Thomas, M. Davies, G. Richards, Revd J. Williams. Front row: Elizabeth Ann Griffiths, L. Morgan, Mrs Griffiths, Vida Griffiths, Revd D.T. Griffiths, V. Thomas, D. Moore, Mrs Morris.

Confirmation Day with Revd Joshua Pritchard Hughes and curates of Llantrisant parish church. Revd Hughes became vicar of Llantrisant in 1883 and was consecrated Bishop of Llandaff in 1905. He resigned in 1931 and died seven years later. A keen supporter of the temperance movement, he established the Red Dragon Temperance Hotel on Heol Sticil y Beddau.

The dedication of two new treble bells by the Bishop of Llandaff on 4 December 1926 which commemorated the completion of the peal of eight bells. Pictured are: 1. Lord Bishop of Llandaff; 2. Revd D.H. Simon, vicar; 3. Revd C. Rees, curate; 4. Revd J.O. Williams, vicar of Gilfach Goch; 5. John Johns vicar's warden; 6. P. Westcott; 7. William Huish, secretary; 8. B. Frances, treble; 9. F. Bryant, deputy leader; 10. W. Westcott; 11. M.H. Davis, peoples warden; 12. R. John; 13. Harry James of Southgate grocery shop and dairy; 14. L. Davis; 15. John Evans, leader; 16. N. Frances; 17. A.E. Powell; 18. Reg Westcott.

Parish church bellringers *c.* 1955. From left to right: Richard Collins, Eddie Davies, Gwyn Westcott, John Evans, William Huish, Brian Westcott, Jack Westcott, Reg Westcott and Mr Rowsell. The original peal of six bells was hung in 1718 and evidence suggests they were actually cast in the tower. When the additional two were added in 1926 a carillon system was also placed in the ringing chamber. All of the bells are inscribed with a dedication to Morgan David and Evan Morgan (1718), Revd James Harries BD (vicar until his death in 1728), Captain Richard Jenkins of Hensol, Taliesin Morgan, John John and Malgwyn H. Davies (1926).

Salem, the Christian Bible chapel on Talbot Road. Fearing persecution, the meetings of early non-conformists were held in secret at remote farms, but the eventual contribution made by the movement to Llantrisant is inestimable. It provided the groundwork through the Sunday schools for people to develop their talents, gave working man the experience of a form of democracy, standards of behaviour were enhanced, a Band of Hope to curb excessive drinking was instigated and the Gymanfa Ganu was born.

Llantrisant showing the rear of the Wesleyan chapel at Southgate. The Welsh-speaking followers of the Wesleyan movement built the original Zozobabel Welsh Wesleyan chapel on Swan Street (opposite the New Inn) in 1813 on the house belonging to Edward William. However, interest waned and by 1896 they failed to appoint trustees. In the next ten years it fell into disuse and was sold to the rural council in 1918. The building was later demolished and the human remains re-interred at Cefn Parc cemetery.

Community Councillor Alcwin Ajax outside the ruin of the Wesleyan chapel, 1980. The English-speaking followers of the Wesleyan movement, who departed from Zozobabel chapel on Swan Street, built this chapel in the spring of 1884. It consisted of two large rooms with a schoolroom that provided the rehearsal hall for the male voice choir. It eventually closed in 1964 and was demolished during the 1990s.

Zoar chapel and Red Dragon Temperance Hall. The original Soar Congregational chapel was built on Cardiff Road, Penygawsi, by disenchanted members of Bethel chapel (later the Church Hall). In 1862 they left Bethel and used rooms at Mwyndy Farm and the Talbot Inn before eventually acquiring the lease of land at Penygawsi. Members later bought Dr Price's old home, Tŷ'r Clettwr, to build the new Zoar in 1902. The Temperance Hotel was opened by vicar Joshua Pritchard Hughes.

Deacons of Zoar chapel in 1959. From left to right, back row: Kenneth Sparnon, Christopher Morgan, Mr Jones (butcher), Gladys (Octavius) Thomas, Revd Stanley Jones, Arthur John. Front row: Annie Sparnon, Beulah Davies, George T. Davies, Evan Llewellyn (Cross Inn). Octavius Thomas worked in a local employment office and according to a local phrase, if anyone was out of work they were on the 'Octi'.

Right: Zoar chapel Annual Report, 1905. Opposite was Trinity Presbyterian church (Elim) built in 1876. Following the influx of English-speaking members to nearby Penuel, separate meetings of Elim were held at Morgan's Hall, a long room at the rear of a dwelling in High Street. In 1897 they secured a deed on the dwelling and demolished it to erect a new house. It was constructed in fine Victorian style and opened in 1898. Elim closed in 1960 to rejoin Penuel with bilingual services.

Below: Swan Street, showing the rear of the church hall which was formerly known as Yr Hen Ty Cwrdd Uchaf, or Bethel chapel and opened by the Welsh Independent movement in 1808. The movement is traced to 1802 with a Revd Griffiths Hughes. In 1851 it had an average Sunday attendance of 421 people, but in 1862 a disagreement broke out and the disenchanted members left for a new meeting place called Soar (or Zoar). In 1902 they re-amalgamated at the new Zoar chapel. Bethel was bought by the parish church and the gallery was removed, but the adjoining cemetery was retained.

⤝ ADRODDIAD ⤛

Eglwys Gynulleidfaol

SOAR, LLANTRISANT,

Am y Flwyddyn 1905.

SWYDDOGION.

GWEINIDOG – PARCH. SAMUEL JONES,

Diaconiaid :

Mr. WILLIAM JOHN.	Mr. JOHN LEWIS.
Mr. OWEN GRIFFITH.	Mr. GEO. T. DAVIES.

Mr. W. OSWAL DAVIES.

Trysorydd yr Eglwys :

Mr. OCTAVIUS THOMAS.

Trysorydd y Drysorfa Adeiladol :

Mr. WILLIAM JOHN.

Ysgrifenydd yr Eisteddleoedd :

Mr. W. OSWAL DAVIES.

Ysgrifenydd :

Mr. GEO. T. DAVIES.

Yr Ysgol Sul :

AROLYGWR	...	Mr. GEO. T. DAVIES.
TRYSORYDD	...	Mr. HENRY JONES.
YSGRIFENYDD	...	Mr. DAVID LLEWELLYN.

CEIDWAD Y CAPEL ... Mrs. LOCK.

55

Quaker meeting house. Known as Tŷ Cwrdd, it was built near a stream at Treferig on the Common. The original members were John Bevan (1636-1729) and his wife Barbara (1637-1710). In 1820 the house was sold for £25 but in 1903 bequeathed by the owner to the Society of Friends. The Treferig Valley Railway was built in 1878 to service the Glyn Colliery and a railway siding existed near Treferig Mill.

Tabor Baptist church and Grabham Butcher's c. 1968. The Baptist movement was first recorded in the town in 1650, but existed amidst great peril of persecution. In 1812 a group met in the Market Hall (the site of the old police station) and a request to the Marquis of Bute to use the town hall was granted.

The congregation of Tabor Baptist on a day trip. Increased membership of the Baptist movement saw them move from the town hall to a house. In 1824, land was acquired at the rear of High Street to build Tabor, which was opened in 1826 and rebuilt in 1924.

A day trip to Porthcawl by the congregations of Zoar and Tabor Baptist chapel *c*. 1942. The man wearing the trilby hat in the centre of the photograph was Luther Jones of Cross Inn, the conductor of Llantrisant Male Voice Choir for fifty-one years.

Penuel Deacons at Ynysallau Farm in 1918. From left to right, back row: Evan Williams, Lewis Williams, Revd Salmon, Morgan Morgan. Front row: Evan Beavan, Richard Morgan, John Morgan, John Morgan. Penuel (Calvinistic Methodist) was built in 1775 and rebuilt 1826. The Methodist movement was first recorded in 1741 at Tŷ Newydd Farm, a mile south of the town. The leader was Thomas William, who drowned in a river in Treorchy in 1753. On 8 February 1775 they secured a lease of a house, stables and garden at Ffynnon Newydd on High Street.

Llantrisant Town School c. 1930. In 1699, Revd James Harries pledged his support for the work of the Society for the Promotion of Christian Knowledge (SPCK) and by 1700 hoped to secure schooling for the poor. In 1701 he established two charity schools and by 1716 had thirty pupils on the roll in a town where parishioners were 'lazy and mutinous' and 'addicted to sports, even in divine service', so he became 'forced to restrain them' against atheism.

Llantrisant Town School from West Caerlan c. 1905. From 1739 to 1773 a circulating school of teachers held classes in the town hall and corn market, patronized by Lord Bute. By 1800 there were three charity schools in Llantrisant, but the system was deplorable. Flogging of boys was widespread, work was ill-prepared and children were insubordinate. One was condemned for 'drawing ludicrous figures on the slate and showing them to the boys'. Following the Education Act of 1870 new schools and school boards were established.

Llantrisant Town School c. 1907. The Llantrisant National School was opened in 1867 and extended in 1897. They were built on West Caerlan, the property of the Earl of Talbot and Shrewsbury who presented the land for the use of the school, which cost £2,000 to build.

Llantrisant Town School 1910. The log books of the school provide fascinating reading. Some of the selections for 1864, when classes were held in the town hall, read, 3 March: 'Howard Ajax absent having his shoes mended'. 18 March: 'Many of the boys absent because of the hunt. Gone after the hounds'. 20 May: 'Gave Robert Bamfield leave for the afternoon to go to the mountain for water for his father'.

Llantrisant Town School staff c. 1927. From left to right, back row: Miss Harris (Gelynog Inn), -?-, Maud West, David Davies, Miss Ethel Jeffreys, -?-, Ceinwen Williams. Front row: Charlotte Morgan (whose daughter, Lottie, was accompanist to Llantrisant Male Choir), headmaster Mr Davies, Mrs Jones and Jimmy Little (father of Peter Little, the postmaster).

Llantrisant Infants School class *c.* 1932. Pupils, from left to right, back row: C. Wall, T. Doster, T. Morgan, G. Williams, O. Finlay, M. Morgan, R. Powell, W. Grother, I. Watkins, K. Jacob, A. Williams, R. Eason, G. Roche, G. Doster. Fourth row: M. Collins, B. John, G. Davies, D. Hall, G. Odgers, L. Dooley, V. Westcott, M. Seary, M. Taylor, B. Morris, N. Stephens, M. James, J. Wyatt. Third row: J. Grother, D. Rees, L. Bryant, C. Aldridge, H. Rees, J. Kingdom, B. Lloyd, I. Harris, D. White, H. Hopkins, M. Thomas, C. Benson, ? Rees, D. Jenkins, G. Dickason. Second row: G. Taylor, R. Wintle, -?-, G. Martin, P. Thomas, V. Causon, L. Davies, G. Hall, J. Kerslake, B. Whalley, M. Doster, K. Clay, D. Gwilyn, W. Jenkins. Front Row: J. Miles, H. Griffiths, H. Williams, E. Harry, N. Westcott, N. Doster, A. Jordan, B. Rees, G. Pope, G. Williams, L. Waters, E. Morris, ? Rees. Teachers are Mrs C. Bissett (left) and Mrs C. Morgan.

Carole (author's mother) and Colin Hooper *c.* 1944. Born in Bristol House on High Street, their parents were collier Arthur Hooper and Gwyneth (formerly Davies), the daughter of Tom 'Butch' Davies. Her sister Blodwyn married Reg Westcott. The Hooper family left Bristol House shortly before it was demolished to widen High Street in 1948, to move to a new home in the newly-built Dan Caerlan council estate.

Children on the steps of the west door of the church following a wedding when the newlyweds carried out the tradition of throwing them pennies, in 1948. From left to right, back row: Fred 'Flyo' Bryant, Colin Hooper. Third row: Iris Stallard, Janet Rees, Dorothy John, Ruth Harrison, -?- (photographer's daughter). Second row: David Davies, Selwyn Charlton, Ainsley Rees, Lyndie Lynn, Pat Evans, Margaret John, Dolly Evans. Front row: Joan Lynn, Anne Stallard, Pauline Davies, Brenda Jenkins, David Bailey, Brynley Thomas, Lorna Evans, Wayne Kendall, Brynley Williams.

Llantrisant children enjoying the benefits of the new playground in Penygawsi in 1949. The photograph includes Betty Lamerton, Jean Rees, Terry Bushby, Mavis Parry, Glynne Holmes, Norman Evans, Marina Evans, Enid Jenkins and baby Mair Jenkins.

Llantrisant School's standard 5 class of April 1956. From left to right, back row: Charles Phillips, Raymond Clay, Melvin Williams, Stephen Rawlings, Neil Gibson, Brian Smith, Glynne Holmes, Barry Jones, Bryn John, Haydn Rees. Middle row: John Foyle, Norman Jones, Diane Griffiths, Yvonne Newton, Patricia John, Jacqueline Land, Gaynor Jenkins, Brian David, Anthony Evans. Front row: Gillian Griffiths, Nesta Mordecai, Anita Chandler, Anne Baker, Sandra Thorne, Gillian Jenkins, Elaine Greenslade, Elizabeth Hurley, Gwyneth Taylor, Valerie Beynon, Patricia Cogbill, Marion Morris.

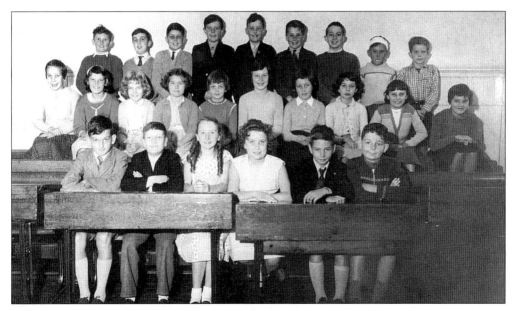

Llantrisant Town School 1958. From left to right, back row: Ryland Griffiths, Alan Turner, Roger Jenkins, Martin Roberts, Derek Richards, David Thomas, Dennis O'Neill, George Bryant (complete with ringworm), Wayne Hutchings. Middle row: Elizabeth Woods, Gaynor Jenkins, Avril Evans, Norma Aldrich, Brenda Bull, Carol Edwards, Christine Phillips, Carol Flower, Georgina Sullivan, Kay Evans. Front row: Robert Ham, Tony Dobbin, Barbara Hurley, Glenys Evans, Brian Dance, Howard Thomas.

Llantrisant Primary School 1968. In September 1974 a new primary school was opened on the woodland near the demolished vicarage and named Coed Yr Esgob (Bishops Wood).

Llantrisant Primary School c. 1972. Four years later and the redundant school on West Caerlan, which closed when Coed yr Esgob was built, opened as a Welsh-medium school named Ysgol Gynradd Gymraeg Llantrisant.

64

Three
Inns and Traders

Thomas James & Sons wheelwrights of Newbridge Road, *c.* 1915. Llantrisant was once a thriving commercial town, boasting markets, fairs, stores and workshops. The most numerous were the leather workers, with glovers, skinners and cordwainers. Also there were carpenters, smiths, clockmakers, butchers, maltsters, innkeepers and food sellers.

Greyhound Inn on the top of Greyhound Lane. Maltsters brewing and retailing ale was the most prosperous business in a town where many families were farmers and pub landlords. Most of the inns were little more than cottage beerhouses and would mostly trade on fair and market days. In 1871 more than twenty-five established public houses were open for business in the old town alone. Malt for the beer was obtained from the Malthouse, but the majority of beerhouses received their supplies from the brewery which was situated in the open space adjacent to the post office on Commercial Street. Residents who kept pigs made a daily visit to the brewery to buy the waste at 1d a bucket.

Fox & Hounds Inn, High Street, during the coronation celebrations of 1911. No mention is made of the pub in the census of 1841, but a decade later the occupant was twenty-five-year-old Daniel Parry of Merthyr Tydfil, who was a coal miner, not an innkeeper. Along with his wife Jane and their two children, they shared the property with a house servant. By 1871 the tenant was Ann Roberts, whose husband Morgan was a local butcher. Undoubtedly Llantrisant enjoyed a dubious reputation for its drunken inhabitants and even in 1854 some of the locals petitioned for Sunday closing.

Wheatsheaf Hotel, High Street, with landlord Edward Morgan (formerly of the Cross Keys and a singer who toured the USA and Canada), wife Annie, daughters Glenys and Elsie, father-in-law James Taylor and Nell the dog. In 1815 it was inherited by Anne Harris from her father, Howell Harris. She married Edward Williams and the property was passed on to their son, Revd David Watkin Williams of Eglwysilan who sold it to Roderick Lewis in 1857 for £450. Lewis died a bachelor in 1897 and the pub was inherited by his sisters, Margaret Bowen and Ellen Lewis, who sold it in 1910 for £1,310 to Edward Morgan (pictured). In 1925 he sold it to the Fern Vale Brewery Company Ltd. It was later home to Llantrisant rugby team and had its own rifle club.

Horse & Groom Hotel (left), next to the Gwalia Stores on High Street. Originally called The Boot, during the 1830s and 1840s, the tenant, Morgan Evans, was also operating a malthouse off High Street belonging to a Mr Harris of Treferig. By 1871 the property was passed on to Thomas David.

Bear Inn, *c.* 1905, while the roof was being replaced. Built in 1780, the pub was next to a blacksmith's forge, and both businesses were run by John (Jack) Williams. Jack 'the Bear' married Rachel Williams, who owned the Star shop. The Star Inn and a few cottages existed almost in the centre of the Bull Ring until the early twentieth century. It was a brewhouse which Joseph John acquired after the death of Revd Owen Jenkins in 1786 and had originally been the house of attorney Henry Morgan, portreeve in 1745. His son, also Joseph John, took it on in 1801 and in 1841 the tenant was stonecutter Joseph Davies. In 1820, along with the Star and White Hart, the Bull Ring was also home to the White Horse and the Irish Harp.

The Williams Family of the Bear Inn *c.* 1895. The father of the family was Henry Williams (died 1908) who took over the pub from his father, Jack 'the Bear'. Henry married Mary Morgan and pictured with newborn baby Daniel are children William Henry, Winifred, Johnny, Theophilus, Marie Louisa, Elim, Asnath and Sinia.

"CROSS KEYS" HOTEL,

LLANTRISANT.

COMMERCIAL AND POSTING HOUSE.

Traps and Carriages on Hire.

WINES AND SPIRITS
OF BEST QUALITY

Cross Keys advertisement, 1898. With such a large amount of public houses, many established in homes, it comes as no surprise that drunken violence was a widespread concern during the Victorian period. In the notoriously dangerous pitched tunnel which led from the Angel on George Street to the White Hart on Swan Street a murder is believed to have taken place. Thomas Harrison, the twenty-year-old son of Dr Harrison of Swan Street was allegedly shot by an Edward Barber of Llantrisant House in 1851. Other sources claim this happened on land close to Newbridge Road.

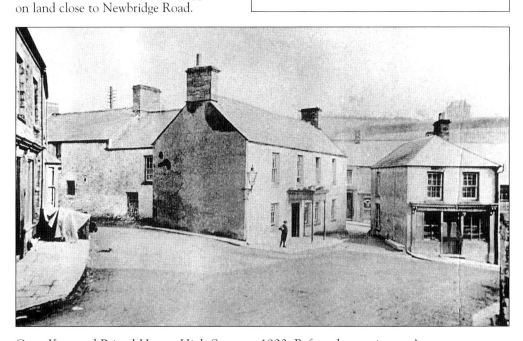

Cross Keys and Bristol House, High Street c. 1900. Before the magistrates' court system was held in the town hall, petty sessions took place in the pub, where the court would meet every alternate Friday during the late nineteenth century. The tenant at the time was Robert Griffiths.

The White Hart pub (demolished 1912), behind County Stores, pictured from Swan Street. At the rear of the pub was a cottage, followed by the George Inn and the pitched alleyway. Hywel Thomas Llywelyn (1714-1764) was one of the earliest innkeepers of the White Hart. It later belonged to R.F. Rickards, whose tenant in 1842 was David Jones, a seventy-year-old widower. He married Catherine William on 18 May 1802 and their youngest daughter, Eleanor, married David Morgan, son of Richard Morgan of the tailor's shop on the Bull Ring. Their son was the future Town Trust clerk and author Taliesin Morgan.

Heol-y-Sarn (Common Road) c. 1910 showing the Welcome to Town pub (bottom left) and the Butchers Arms (top right). The Butchers was originally an old coaching inn, first referred to in 1792 when Richard David, a cordwainer, became tenant. His widow continued after his death until 1802. Prior to that it was large house, taxed at 10s, belonging to Thomas Williams, officer of excise. In 1900 it became the home of Gwenllian Llywelyn and her children Penelopen and Nicholas (children of Dr Price) until East Caerlan House was built in 1906.

The George Inn, Swan Street. It once belonged to a dynasty of aldermen possessing estates in Llanwynno and Aberdare. At one time it was a stable and court and belonged to Phillip Williams in 1753 and eventually passed down to John Jenkins (1796-1860) the diarist, who owned six houses on Swan Street and ran the pub until 1855. Mr Jenkins converted a house on Swan Street into a malthouse in 1830. He later sold it to Morgan Thomas in 1848 for £124. In 1912 the two inns and intervening cottages were demolished and replaced by the union workhouse, but the pitched alleyway remained.

New Inn, Swan Street. Once the property of Jesus College Oxford, from 1762 to 1782 the occupier was Jennet William and her father, maltster Richard William. From 1796 to 1815 the tenant was Thomas Llewellyn, who married Jennet in 1778 (she died 1792). Llywelyn's father, Hywel Thomas Llywelyn, was innkeeper of the White Hart. Thomas Llewellyn stayed in the New Inn until his death from drunkenness in 1815, when he was succeeded by his son-in-law David Shephard (1777-1837). His daughter, also Jennet, and her farmer husband Richard Morgan continued there. From 1851 the New Inn was owned by William Williams, who married Susannah, daughter of Richard Morgan of the Swan Fach. Their daughter, Mary, married Samuel Spencer, who was landlord in 1871.

Left: Shrewsbury Hotel, Newbridge Road, c. 1916. The pub stood between three cottages (to the left) and two houses (towards the Cross Keys), along with a garage used for Thomas James & Sons wheelwrights firm on the opposite side of the road. One of the first landlords was John Hughes, followed by William Thomas in 1871. When Newbridge Road was widened between 1934 and 1937 the entire row of buildings was demolished.

Below: Llantrisant Inn, Heol-y-Sarn, the landlord of which, according to the 1871 census, was Thomas John. The pub stood opposite the Butcher's Arms and was later converted into two houses.

The original Llantrisant Workingmen's Club was opened in the former Rock & Fountain Inn on the Bull Ring in May 1953. It moved to a new building on the site of the former Rickards Arms (called the Five Courts until 1840) on Swan Street by 1956, where the ancient game of five courts was played. Pictured, from left to right: Charlie Evans, Sammy Davies, Tommy John, Trevor Evans, Bill 'Cowboy' Jenkins (kneeling), David Long, Dilwyn 'Mickey' Montague, Charlie Williams, Ivor Watkin.

Committee and officers at the opening of the Workingmen's Club's new extension, 28 September 1961. From left to right, back row: Cyril Harrison, Lyndon Groves. Middle row: Ken Booth, Mervyn Collins, Tom Bryant, Evan Harry, C. Harrison, D. Bendle, William Maslin, Cliff O'Neill. Front row: Ivor Ginger Watkins, C. Williams, Viv Williams, Mr Ausden, Gordon Jenkins, David Edwards, Llew Harrison.

A group of wives in the Cross Keys c. 1971. Pictured, from left to right, back row: Anne Evans, Janice Griffiths, Betty Green, Mary Alexander. Middle row: Beverley Westcott, Maria Dominico, Emily Griffiths, Mabel Dooley, Pam Mounter, Cath Griffiths, Bronwen Selwood. Front row: Patricia John and Dorothy John.

Llantrisant RFC clubhouse, built by a local company headed by Alun Rees, opened in 1973. Dubbed the Black Army, possibly due to the valour showed by longbowmen at the battle of Crecy in 1346, Llantrisant rugby team originally played on the field which later became Dan Caerlan estate (owned by Mr John). Cefn Mabley fields were later adopted as the home turf and the clubhouse followed, although until then players used the Wheatsheaf Hotel.

William Bryant (1760-1833), painted in 1786 while delivering glass to Cardiff. A local glazier, he married Mary Robert, a Freeman's daughter and he became a Freeman in 1807. The couple had nine children, one of whom – called William – also became a glazier and lived on High Street. His daughter married David Llewellyn, who owned the butcher's shop on the Bull Ring (later County Stores).

Southgate Turnpike c. 1895. Commercially, Llantrisant began to falter during the late nineteenth century due to the growing prosperity of neighbouring Pontypridd (Newbridge). Markets and fairs gradually declined but shops and permanent workshops thrived for another two generations.

A coal delivery at Harry James's grocery business on the Southgate in the 1920s. James also ran his dairy business with a hand-trolley, a method inherited by his successor Mervyn Collins in 1944, who later launched Collins Dairies in Cross Inn.

Mervyn Collins (born 1930) pushing Robin Hughes and Gary Wynne in his first handcart used for delivering milk c. 1947. In 1942 he worked for Harry James before taking over the milk round with his older brother Layton in 1943. Following his brother's death, Mervyn moved the business to Cross Inn Road, and during the next fifty years Collins Dairies prospered, allowing 'Collins the Milk' to open new dairies in Cross Inn for his fleet of twenty milk floats.

Southgate Toll House, better known as the Turnpike House, which once stood opposite the Southgate bend on the lower end of High Street c. 1898. The turnpike roads were set up by an Act of Parliament in 1756 but were declared main roads in 1878. In 1851 Thomas Williams, a farmer of 10 acres was tenant. Tolls were imposed on goods entering the town for sale on market days and fairs, and were used to help repair the baronial roads, bridges and the town walls.

Northgate Cottage, Heol-y-Sarn. Owned by Llantrisant Town Trust, the tenant from 1906 was Edwin Francis, succeeded by Clydai Evans (1883-1954) from April 1920 whose brothers were Iestyn, Johnny and Ithel Evans. She remained in the house until a burglary by two Rhondda men forced her to leave and the last known resident of the cottage before it was demolished in the late 1950s was Freda Williams.

GLAMORGANSHIRE.

LANTRISAINT WORK-HOUSE, *May* 11th, 1784.

TO the End of rendering a more humane Treatment of the Poor, and an Eafe of a Load of Taxes on the Parifhioners :---By feveral Refolutions of the Parifhioners, and being countenanced therein by an ACT of PARLIAMENT, the faid HOUSE has been eftablifhed on the following Plan:

FIRST,

THE Parifhioners, at their feveral Veftries, have nominated and appointed fuch of the Parifhioners as are moft likely to have a lafting Intereft in the faid Parifh, to be Truftees of the faid Houfe and of the Poor therein, in Order to attend on the fame, and do their Endeavour to fee it anfwer the Ends propofed.

II. THE faid Truftees (for the obtaining of that End) are to meet every *Friday*, at the Governor's Room in the faid Work-houfe, between 10 o'Clock in the Morning and 2 in the Afternoon, to perufe the Accounts of Receipts and Expenditure, and alfo to confider of the beft Means to promote the Intereft of the faid Houfe and the Poor therein.

III. THE Rates charged on the Parifh are to be delivered into the Hands of *one* of the *Overfeers*, or fome other proper Perfon, who for that Year is to be appointed by the Truftees to be the *Treafurer*; and he is to purchafe with the fame every Neceffary for the faid Houfe, according to the Direction of the Truftees, and he is alfo to produce weekly an Account of all Sums of Money received or expended by him, with the proper Vouchers for the fame. And the faid Truftees are to perufe, approve of, and fettle the faid Accounts, at the faid Veftry or weekly Meeting.

IV. THE Account of all Receipts and Difburfements fhall be fairly entered in a Book to be made and kept for that Purpofe; which Book, and the Accounts therein, all the Parifhioners, or either of them, (who pay Poor-Rates) may be at Liberty to infpect or perufe in the Governor's-Room, in the faid Work-houfe, at fuch Time, and as often as he or they may think proper.

V. THE faid *Treafurer* is to have fuch Sum, for his Trouble in fo doing, as the faid Truftees, in a Veftry, fhall agree upon.

VI. IN all Matters requiring the Determination of the *Truftees*, it fhall be conftrued, that the major Part of fuch of them as fhall be affembled at the faid Veftry, fhall determine all Matters in Difpute.

The appointed BILL of FARE.

BREAD to be made of mixed *Wheat* and Barley.			
May	Breakfaft.	Dinner.	Supper.
11 *Tuefday*	Milk-Porridge	Beef and Roots	Broth
12 *Wednefday*	Broth	Flummery and Milk	Milk-Porridge
13 *Thurfday*	Milk-Porridge	Beef or Mutton and Roots	Broth
14 *Friday*	Broth	Flummery and Milk	Milk-Porridge
15 *Saturday*	Milk-Porridge	Bread & Butter with Roots	Milk-Porridge
16 *SUNDAY*	Milk-Porridge	Beef and Roots	Broth
17 *Monday*	Broth	Bread and Cheefe with Beer	Milk-Porridge

To breakfaft at Eight, *dine at* Two, *and fup at* Eight.

VII. No Poor to be admitted but by the Truftees at their weekly Veftry.

VIII. THAT the appointed Bill of Fare be punctually obferved.

IX. THAT every of the Poor be examined, and wafhed clean, at entering into the Houfe, and get what Clothaes as fhall be neceffary according to the Directions of the Truftees.

X. THAT the upper Garment of the Poor be of the fame Colour, and badged with the Letters L. P. in Red.

XI. No Poor to be permitted to go out of Doors, otherwife than on neceffary Occafions, and by Leave of the Governor.

XII. THAT all the Poor who are able to work, fhall attend at their Work from *Six* in the Morning to *Seven* in the Evening, from *Lady*-Day to *Michaelmas*; and from *Seven* in the Morning to *Six* in the Evening, from *Michaelmas* to *Lady*-Day, excepting Half-an-hour for Breakfaft, and One for Dinner.

XIII. IF any to avoid Work, plead Ailment, they are to be properly examined by the Doctor who attends the Houfe, and the Governor therein; and if it fhall appear that they make falfe Excufes, or if they fhall not behave peaceably, quietly, and fubmiffively, they fhall be punifhed with the Lofs of their firft Meal of Meat; and if they *perfift* in any Mifconduct, they fhall be treated with the Rigour of Law, and fent to the Houfe of Correction.

XIV. THE Governor to order the Poor into feparate Divifions of 2 or 3, as may be moft eligible for Work; and weigh whatever Wool is given to each Divifion for fpinning, and alfo weigh the fame when in Yarn; and produce the fame (the Work of each Divifion feparate) unto the Truftees at their weekly Veftry or Meeting.

XV. THE Governor alfo to advife the Truftees, at their weekly Meeting, with proper Information, required by the faid Truftees, in Regard of any Matter refpecting the Provifions, Materials or Employment of the Poor in the faid Houfe, or of any other Matter in Regard of the faid Houfe or the Poor therein, or in any Ways concerning the fame.

XVI. THAT the Rooms of the faid Houfe be kept clean, and fwept or wafhed every *Tuefday*, *Thurfday* and *Saturday*. That the Windows be frequently left open, that Wormwood be ufed to fumigate the Rooms, to wafh the Linnen, and to lay in the Beds.

XVII. THAT the Children be wafhed and combed regularly every Morning, by fome Perfon or Perfons appointed for that Purpofe.

XVIII. THAT fome Portion in the Old or New Teftament be read in the Work-houfe every Evening immediately after *Seven* o'Clock, and that the Poor therein do attend on the fame.

XIX. IT is alfo recommended, that the Poor (fuch as be able) do every *Sunday* attend at the Church, or fome other Place of Public Worfhip, or on reading the *Scriptures*.

XX. THAT the Youth be kept at School until fuch Time as they are able to work, and then fet to Work; either in the faid Houfe, or be apprenticed out.

XXI. THAT for the Encouragement and Inducement of the Poor to Induftry, every Divifion of 2 or 3 as before-mentioned fhall receive, for every Pound of Wool they fhall card and fpin, the Sum of Two-pence, (half thereof to the Spinner) and every *other Work* rewarded *in like Proportion*; and a Lift of fuch Divifion, and their Proportion of Work, as alfo the feparate Work of other Individuals to be delivered by the Governor unto the Truftees at their weekly Meeting, in Order that they may be fatisfied that the Poor are properly employed. --- But if either of the faid *Divifions*, or an Individual, fhall prove to be *indolent* and not induftrious *according to* (his or their) *Ability*, the faid *Encouragement* Money fhall be withdrawn from fuch Divifion or Individual, until fuch Time as the Governor fhall certify his or their Induftry to the Truftees at their weekly Meeting.

XXII. THE Poor in the faid Houfe may expend the Money fo granted unto them, (for *Encouragement*) in fuch Ways and Means as they think moft proper.

XXIII. No Perfon in the faid Workoufe, on any Account, is to fmoke in a Bed-Room or Up-ftairs.

XXIV. IT fhall be allowed for the Governor to vary in the Rules of Diet, herein before prefcribed, into Apples and Milk, Rice and Milk, Apple-dumplins, Apple-pudding, Rice-pudding, *&c.* provided the major Part of the Poor apply for fuch Change of Diet, and the major Part of the Truftees at their weekly Meeting approve of the fame.

LASTLY, The Truftees, at their weekly Meeting, fhall from Time to Time advife and adopt fuch *further* Regulations, Rules and Orders, as they may judge moft beneficial for promoting the Ends propofed in eftablifhing the faid Houfe.

(CARMARTHEN, PRINTED BY J. ROSS, IN LAMMAS-STREET.)

Llantrisant workhouse regulations. A vestry meeting was held on 5 December 1783 to consult in regard of establishing a workhouse for the poor. Vagabonds, prostitutes and thieves were rife in the town. Margaret Jenkins, a widow, was engaged as superintendent to see the poor fed, put to work and weigh and measure every article used in the said house, for which she was paid £12 a year, fire, meat, candles and one room for her use. On 5 May 1784 it was unanimously resolved to open the workhouse, the first in Glamorgan, in a block of adapted cottages in Swan Street owned by Revd Gervase Powell of Llanharan, and for a short time in the Black Cock Inn on Yr Allt. It was decided to borrow money from Revd Rickards and his trustees to pay for the initial costs. The vestry agreed the sum of £120 but workhouse treasurer Joseph John took £430. Terrified by John's violent behaviour, the vicar appealed to the Court of Great Sessions for protection because John had tried to induce various people to blow him up, run over him with a wagon, startle his horse, or otherwise dispose of him. John was sentenced to transportation and died in the hulks at Portsmouth. By the late nineteenth century the union workhouse was opened at the rear of County Stores to accommodate the ever-growing populace of paupers.

Market day, c. 1890. Fairs and markets probably occurred as far back as the thirteenth century as an outlet of the agricultural surplus of the area. Four fairs were held annually on 1 May, 13 May, 1 August and 18 October, while Friday was market day. Adjoining the town hall was the corn market (later the police station) and a square was formed with stalls on each side, arranged in rows with each one given a name. The new community of Newbridge – later Pontypridd – rapidly established itself as a rival to the old borough.

Bull Ring c. 1890, showing the Star buildings on the right. The bulls were tied by their noses to a circle of iron inset into a large stone and cattle were auctioned by the local farmers. The square was for bull-baiting, using a breed of white terrier, but this was disallowed in 1827 because it was encouraging unruly crowds. Cattle often broke loose, and there are accounts of people scrambling to the roofs of their cottages to escape the beasts, while watching the event with an atmosphere reminiscent of a Roman amphitheatre.

Collwyn Davies (1916-1991) and his sister Margaret Florence May (1914-1936) were the children of Thomas Hopkin Davies (1888-1952) and May Elizabeth Davies (1893-1967) of Swan Street. They ran a grocery shop on the Bull Ring, previously known as the Bee Hive and later to become Edith Dyer's sweet shop. Eventually the couple bought Crown Stores on High Street, and would travel around neighbouring communities in a horse and cart selling ice cream.

County Stores, Bull Ring. On the right of the picture is the Rock & Fountain Inn, traced back to 1782 when it was a large property belonging to Patrick Aherne Owen. By 1896 it was owned by William Hudson and John Edmund, and it later became the town's first working men's club in May 1953.

County Stores and the town pump on the Bull Ring *c.* 1960. Many pumps and wells exist in the town, with the town pump and that on Newbridge Road still remaining. Under the protection of the Town Trust, the town pump well was deepened in September 1826 and repaired by the Portreeve. In 1889 the Town Trust paid £1 to Mary David to clean and take care of it. Due to frequent epidemics, little use was made of it by the beginning of the twentieth century.

Bull Ring, August 1971. The County Stores was demolished and a nuts and bolts factory, followed by a glove-making factory, was established in its place. One of the workers, Tonyrefail-born Iris Williams became an international singer. It was later used as the studios for the HTV serial *Taff Acre* during the 1980s.

John David demolishing the cottages on the corner of Swan Street and Heol y Sarn, 1903. Better known as 'Johnny White Hart', his mother Mary Ann, landlady of the White Hart pub, died in 1886 and he ran it with his brother William until 1900. The pub fell into ruin and was demolished in 1912. Here he is pictured demolishing three cottages to make way for a butcher's shop and two new cottages. It soon became obvious that the sun shone in the direction of the front window of the new butcher's shop, ruining the produce. In 1914 he bought a shop (in the shade) on the opposite side of the Bull Ring and the original butcher's became a fish and chip shop.

'Johnny White Hart' David (1868-1949) pictured outside the butcher's shop which he occupied on the Bull Ring from 1914. He married Mary Louisa Williams (1878-1910), whose father was Henry Williams, landlord of the Bear. He bought this shop from Hannah Watkins, the local seamstress, and it was later passed down to his daughter Mary David, who worked there along with her brother John, who died in 1959. She kept the business going alone until decimalization in 1970. Next door was Edith Dyer's sweet shop.

High Street, 1900, prior to East Caerlan House being built in 1906. High Street and Commercial Street were home to such stores as Sparnan's grocers, Tamplin's butchers, Clay's barbers, Spenser's barbers, Rees' bakers, Bon Marché (men's outfitters), Gwalia Stores (grocers), Penny Bazaar, and Thomas & Evans.

High Street c. 1940, showing Bristol House, a group of homes occupied by Mrs Jenkins, Mrs Harvey and the Hoopers, which was demolished to make room for a new road leading to the Bull Ring in 1948. Until then only a narrow lane existed to the right of this picture, with a junction on to Commercial Street called Gwt Bach. During the late nineteenth century it was a notorious place for drunks and prostitutes.

Commercial Street showing the Cross Keys, grocer's store, 'paper shop' and the post office in January 1974. For many years Edith Griffiths ran the grocery store to the left of the picture, while the main shop in the centre sold confectionery and daily newspapers. It was run by a host of different families whose names included Jones, Isaacs and Davies. Prior to it being known as the 'paper shop' it was often referred to as the Maypole.

Llantrisant post office, April 1970. The building was chosen as the first telephone exchange, run by James Little (born 1871). In March 1928 the clerk to the Town Trust was instructed by the postmaster general in London to establish the exchange and call it Pontyclun Telephone Exchange since so many of the parish council lived outside Llantrisant. Regarding the naming as a slight on the town, the Trustees unanimously agreed that the name of Llantrisant be used and pressurised the postmaster general in the strongest terms. On 19 May 1928 the Llantrisant Telephone Exchange was officially named and opened.

Lyons' Tea delivery to County Stores on Bull Ring. Other shops in the immediate vicinity included Manchester House (linen and cloth), Nottingham House (books and shoes), Bristol House (flour and corn) London House (china and glass). By 1914 it was also home to Sladen Sweets and Shoe Repairs, Lloyd's Bank, Bee Hive sweet shop, John David (butcher's) and a fish and chip shop owned by Mr Davies, whose son Trevor adopted the nickname 'Chippo'.

Yr Allt c. 1910. The Black Cock Inn building is pictured to the left, backing on to the churchyard wall. Originally the pub was run by the Matthews family of Y Rhws and Aberaman and was later occupied by Watkin Evans, the surgeon. By 1784 it was used as a workhouse, but eventually changed into two or three cottages in 1804. The parish offices, centre, were opened in 1865.

John Morgan (1829-1926) and Marie Morgan (formerly David, 1827-1910). Mrs Morgan lived in the Tennis Courts (later Dan y Castell) and started baking bread before making beer in 1865 when the Cornish miners opened Ynysplwm pit and the Ely railway line. In 1870 John Morgan bought the land behind the Wheatsheaf for £1,000 and built Roam Road. Together they opened Morgan's Bakers. The business passed to their son Daniel Morgan, who fell ill, and his sister, Margaret Morgan (later Rees) ran the business. Another sister, Mary, married Henry Williams, landlord of the Bear.

Margaret Rees (formerly Morgan) (1870-1957) and Richard Rees (1868-1957). Richard Rees was born in South Cornelly and came to Llantrisant to establish a carpentry business and wheelwrights with contracts to build houses during the First World War. By April 1918 he joined his wife to run the bakehouse. Their daughter, Margaret (born 1908) married Stuart David (1904-1993), son of 'Johnny White Hart', who came to work in the bakehouse in 1917 and was one of the first master bakers to graduate from Cardiff Technical College.

Eunice Rees (1898-1977) and John Rees (1899-1927) pictured at the bakehouse. Their parents were Margaret and Richard Rees, who ran the bakery before it was passed to their sister Margaret and her husband, Stuart David.

Stuart David, Willy Rees and Danny Mead pictured with the delivery vans of the Bakehouse in 1926. The bakery existed in this form until 1951 when the introduction of sliced bread destroyed the business. Instead they continued as corn merchants and suppliers of animal food.

Collwyn Davies (1916-1991) the well-known shopkeeper, outside Bradford House, High Street, c. 1970. Better known as Collwyn Lloyd (after his grandmother's maiden name), he followed in his parents' footsteps by running the grocery shop on the Bull Ring. After serving in the army in Singapore during the Second World War he married Margaret Eleanor Griffiths and the couple had three children. Collwyn occupied County Stores on the Bull Ring, a particularly popular shop during the festive period when he sold hundreds of Christmas trees. In later years he opened a bookmaker's nearby before occupying the former Silkstone's drapery at Bradford House, followed by Crown Stores (originally his parents' store) on High Street.

Viv Rees (later clerk to the Town Trust) pictured outside his grocery shop along with his assistant and delivery boy on High Street, c. 1950. During the early part of the century, Charlie Usher of Cardiff would sell fish in a nearby shed, which was only lit by flares.

Thomas Williams of the Red Dragon Temperance Hotel on his milk float in Swan Street, c. 1919. Swan Street was once home to the Brewery Tap, George Inn, New Inn, Rock & Fountain Inn and the Rickards Arms. The most significant was the Swan Fach, dating back to the eighteenth century and left by Mrs Ffriswith Pritchard on 10 May 1757 to be leased by carpenter William Aubrey for a 999-year lease at the annual rent of £5. He sold it to Thomas Austin and David Morgan in 1802 for £90 and by 1818 it was a multiple tenancy.

Swan Street Stores, c. 1890. In 1869 the grocery and drapery shop flourished under the guidance of George Morgan, son of shoemaker William Morgan. It was later inherited by George's daughter Anne (1846-1911) who married collier John David (1846-1903). Their son William Morgan David (1880-1952) inherited the property and following the death of his first wife, Mati Griffiths in 1908, he concentrated solely on the business. In 1920 he married Priscilla Hopkins (1896-1961) who passed the shop on to his son, also William Morgan David (1921-1995).

Amelia Watkins (1896-1991) of Heol y Sarn. Her sister Celia (1896-1979) milked cows and Amelia delivered the produce throughout the town. For a time she also delivered the morning post on horseback to remote farms. Her first husband, Charles Henry Norris (1888-1926), died after contracting a disease while serving in the armed forces in India. She later married William John Rees (1908-2001). Amelia's third sister, Harriet (1901-1980), married Harry Alexander of Cae Ysgubor Farm on Heol y Sarn.

Les Croft (on the right) and David John Griffiths, pictured on Bull Ring Farm c. 1930. 'Crofty' was an accomplished huntsman and horseman who also played rugby for Llantrisant during his youth. David (Dai Fat) Griffiths (b. 1911), was a well-known stonemason. He was one of the eleven children of Isaiah and Jenny Griffiths of the fish and chip shop on Newbridge Road and, like five of his brothers, served in the armed forces, in his case the Royal Artillery. He became a Freeman in May 1934. His last major undertaking was building the large wall to the rear of the Cross Keys public house.

Thomas David, also known as Gwydd-Weaver, the town crier (1846-1906). The arrival of essential food supplies during periods of shortage was announced by the town crier, who also announced newsworthy items. His successor was William Jewell of St Davids Place and the practice continued until the late 1930s.

The town hall and police station, October 1913. The police force in Glamorgan dates from 1839, when each officer had to be below forty years of age and stand over 5ft 7ins tall without shoes. He had to be able to read, write and keep accounts, but could not be a pub landlord, gamekeeper, bailiff or parish clergyman. In January 1840, Thomas Morgan Lewis became Llantrisant's superintendent, with six constables – one was James Hume, who lived on the Bull Ring. In 1848 Llantrisant enjoyed a sergeant's station with PC Rees Rowlands as constable. At one time the station was located in Swan Street, but a new one was built in 1876 on the site of the old corn market. Until then prisoners were kept in a cell in the castle.

Llantrisant and Llantwit Fardre fire crew. With the ever-growing communities of Beddau, Tynant and Talbot Green nearby, a fire crew was established by the start of the twentieth century. At one time an ambulance station also existed on the Bull Ring.

Collecting hay off Gwaun Ruperra fields c. 1920. Notice the rear of Newbridge Road behind them. Under the 1851 census the road is known as Rhiwperrau, but was better known as Cardiff Row, and had the reputation of being one of the toughest areas in the town.

Thomas Albert Davies (left) of Newbridge Road (1877-1960). Better known as Tom 'Butch', he was born in Nantymoel and came to Llantrisant after marrying Margaret Rees of Cefn y Mabley Farm in 1898. Enjoying a notorious reputation as a pig slaughterer, he would undertake the work at farms in the area, but could only find the courage to kill the animals if he was drunk. It was not uncommon for Tom to kill the animals and make off with various organs without the farmer's knowledge. According to the sign in the background, when this photograph was taken there was no beer about.

Isaiah Griffiths (1881-1962) at his fish and chip shop at 27 Newbridge Road during the 1930s. His wife was Jennie (1887-1967) and they had seven boys and four girls called Megan, David (later known as Dai Fat), Ivor, Eileen, Tudor, Muriel, Myra, Vivian, Thomas, William and Howell.

Arthur (1910-1974), and Gwyneth Hooper (1911-1996), grandparents of the author, who were married in St Illtyd's church, Llantwit Fardre in 1935, pictured with friends and relatives on Commercial Street around 1939. Arthur Hooper, of Treforest, spent most of his working life in the Cwm Colliery and also played E flat bass in Llantrisant Town Band shortly after marrying Gwyneth Davies, daughter of Tom 'Butch' Davies.

Brynteg House, September 1936. At one time the house was used as a hospital for handicapped children, who usually came from wealthy families in Cardiff. The nurse in the centre of the picture is Gwyneth Davies, aged seventeen. One of the three Davies sisters of Heol y Sarn (Common Road), she later married Ron Cale and settled in Swan Street.

Four
Custom and Culture

Freemen on the Beating of the Bounds ceremony, marching down High Street from the Bull Ring, June 1946. Clerk to the Town Trust, Stanley Thomas, is holding the seventeenth-century borough mace, older than the one in the House of Commons.

The Llantrisant Charter granted by Richard Beauchamp, Earl of Warwick in the reign of Henry VI, on 29 October 1424. The belief that charters were granted by Gwrgan ap Ithel, the Welsh Lord of Glamorgan in 994 to allow the townsmen the liberties and freedom of the common lands, called Cymdda Fawr and Cymdda Bach and the Graig, is pure speculation. However on 4 March 1346 the first known charter was granted by Edward III through Hugh Despenser.

Llantrisant Town Trust, 1890. The original Trustees were appointed for life and held their first meeting on 31 January 1890. They were: John Evans, Roderick Lewis, Evan John, Josiah Lewis, Joseph Davies, William John, Thomas Llewellyn, Taliesin Morgan, John Treharne, John Thomas and David Evans, the Lord Mayor of London. Surprisingly enough, one Court Leet meeting was actually held in the Mansion House in London!

Corporate Property poster, December 1887. From 1424 to 1889 Llantrisant was a municipal borough, or corporate town. Under the Municipal Corporation Act, the borough was dissolved and became part of a wider administration. The dissolution brought into being the Llantrisant Town Trust, an elected group of Trustees established under the Board of Charity Commissioners on 17 December 1889, to manage the common lands. As a free borough, it was a community of Freemen (burgesses) and its main purpose was to earn a corporate living. It was a trading and business community and to help it succeed in a competitive world its burgesses gathered a range of privileges giving them a measure of self government, their own courts of law and control on markets and fairs.

CHARITY COMMISSION.

LLANTRISANT CORPORATE PROPERTY.

"Municipal Corporations Act. 1883."

By direction of the Board of Charity Commissioners for England and Wales, Notice is hereby given that ARTHUR CARDEW, Esq., Barrister-at-Law, Assistant Commissioner, will open a

PUBLIC INQUIRY

for the purposes of the above named Act, at Ten o'clock in the Forenoon, of Tuesday, the 6th day of December, 1887, at the

TOWN HALL, LLANTRISANT.

Charity Commission,
Whitehall, S.W.
23rd November, 1887.

Signed,
D. R. FEARON.

Beating of the Bounds, 25 August 1930. Freemen were granted the complex definition of sacred cattle (not sheep) rights to the common lands in four ways: by marriage, birth, apprenticeship or gift. Other privileges included selling merchandise without paying fees or tolls, while promising to protect the town. Today, a Freeman is anyone aged twenty-one or over and either the son of a Freeman or married to a Freeman's daughter (a petticoat Freeman), and is inaugurated at the annual Court Leet held in the town hall.

Freemen and local school children on the Castle Green in June 1946. On the 600th anniversary since Llantrisant was presented with its first Charter, the children sang a specially-arranged song written to the tune of 'God Bless the Prince of Wales', which opened with the lines: 'Llantrisant On A Mountain, Smiles o'er Morgannwg's Vales. It gave to mighty London, A real Lord Mayor from Wales'.

Llantrisant Town Trustees on the Castle Green, June 1946, with Clerk Stanley Thomas. Trustees overcame the furore within the Town Trust a year earlier where a series of forged cheques had been discovered, and an investigation involving the Charity Commission held.

Beating of the Bounds, June 1946. Pictured from left to right are Dennis Regan, Colin Hooper, James Edward Harrison, Mr Sparnon, Viv Rees and Bronwen Elizabeth Harrison. With the formation of the Town Trust in 1889, a Seal was designed by Mr Drane of Cardiff, representing the arms of Despenser (left), de Clare (centre) and Robert Consul (right).

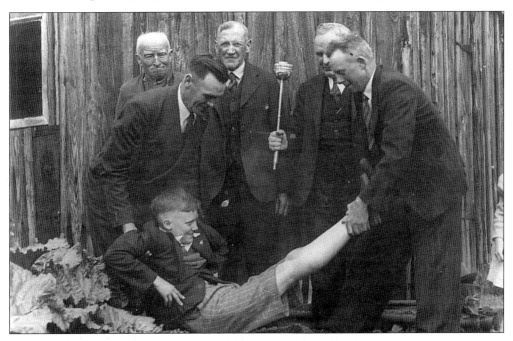

Reg Wescott and Harry Alexander bumping Keith Rowlands on a boundary stone in Cross Inn, during the Beating of the Bounds in June 1946. Children and young men not yet admitted as Freemen were dropped on their buttocks on the boundary stones to impress in their minds the ancient landmarks. Will Rees is holding the mace in the background.

Beating of the Bounds leaving the parish church, 19 June 1954. Following a civic service in the parish church conducted by Revd J.J. Thomas, the Beating of the Bounds began. The religious custom dates back to the ninth century, but is first recorded in Llantrisant in 1555. Held every seven years or so, Freemen would exercise the right to walk the seven mile boundary of the Ancient Borough to defend the area where they enjoyed the rights of the land.

Beating of the Bounds, town hall steps, 19 June 1954. The mace is dated 1633 and has a Charles I five shilling piece implanted in the head. It is older than the Mace in the House of Commons and has been carried in the ancient town for 350 years. Now it is only used at the annual Court Leet.

Beating of the Bounds, 19 June 1954. The formal Civic Procession for this event was led by a police car from the old town to Cross Inn. It escorted the Band of the 5th Battalion, the Welsh Regiment TA, followed by Superintendent A. Morris and Inspector R. Richins. The clerk and Town Trust members followed, along with the Lord Lieutenant and dignitaries from the Glamorgan County Council and Llantrisant and District Rural Council.

Beating of the Bounds at Cross Inn, 19 June 1954. A number of other dignitaries from neighbouring councils also participated in the first section of the boundary walk. They included representatives of Cardiff, Cowbridge and Barry, along with Llantrisant Trades Council, Parish Council, the Archers and Freemen, with positions even reserved for Penelopen Price, Madeline Elsas, Tudor John and Cyril Lewis.

Freemen and Trustees pictured on the Castle Green following the Court Leet at the Guild Hall *c.* 1960. Two years earlier the Town Trust purchased the eighteenth-century town hall and it is regularly used by the Court Leet. It was rebuilt in 1773 by the Marchioness of Bute – Lady Windsor – for the sum of £100, due to a fall in the market's popularity. The hall served as the town's first National School before becoming home to a bi-weekly magistrates' court (until the court opened in Talbot Green in 1957).

Freemen and Trustees of Llantrisant on the steps of the town hall following the Court Leet of May 1966. Colonel Sir Cennydd Traherne, Lord Lieutenant of Glamorgan who became a Trustee in 1955, is pictured at front along with the clerk, Viv Rees.

Residents of Llantrisant enjoyed a dinner at the town hall as part of Queen Victoria's Golden Jubilee celebrations, Wednesday 30 June 1897. At first the town was unsure how to celebrate the occasion, although a clock was almost installed in the church tower. A huge bonfire was lit on West Caerlan, by Master Norman Hughes (vicarage) and Master Dunn of Crofta House. The Masters family of Lanelay entertained 900 children for tea and gave each one a penny.

Llantrisant Wax Works 1898. The similarity to modern waxworks extended no further than the costumes worn by the characters represented. They assumed the likeness of Weary Will, Tired Tim, Funny Tom and the Emperor of Japan. The waxworks were part of the St David's Day celebrations, in which the Llantrisant Male Voice Party entertained.

Private Warrington receiving the Military Medal for his bravery during the First World War, town hall, 1916. The man at the front is the town crier William Jewell, and to the right is Penelopen Price dressed in her Red Cross nurse's outfit. Also pictured is Dai 'The Post' Rees, a postman for thirty-three years who was denied a pension because his job was considered temporary. The local MP took his case to the High Court to ensure he received a full pension.

Private William Dooley receiving the Distinguished Conduct Medal on the steps of the town hall, 1916. Penelopen Price is pictured once more to the left of the war hero.

Sergeant Ivor Davies, of Newbridge Road, a soldier in the Welsh Regiment, decorated with the Distinguished Conduct Medal at the town hall in 1916 for conspicuous gallantry and devotion to duty. According to the address, 'He commanded his platoon with great skill during rearguard action and tried his utmost to rescue his wounded officer when the enemy were within fifty yards'. Also pictured are his wife Elizabeth Davies and their baby John, town crier William Jewel and Canon Griffiths presenting the medal.

James Taylor, Lord Mayor of Cardiff and Freeman of Llantrisant, visiting the town hall for a civic reception, and possibly to receive his Freeman's roll on 21 May 1921. His father, also James Taylor, is pictured on the right of the picture wearing a hat and a white beard. The Lord Mayor's sister, Annie, married Edward Morgan, landlord of the Wheatsheaf Hotel.

Children collecting for the Soldiers' and Sailors' Fund on the top of High Street, 1916. Many Llantrisant men lost their lives during the two world wars and memorial plaques were unveiled on the interior walls of the parish church.

Llantrisant Soldiers' and Sailors' Reception Committee issued this picture, which was taken from the steps of the town hall in 1916, for the princely sum of 6d. The rear of the picture stated: 'Purchasers of this card could win top prizes in a raffle: 1st prize Goose (£1); 2nd prize Duck (10/-); 3rd prize cigars (5/-)'.

The bonfire on the Graig was one of the highlights of the two-day festival to commemorate King George VI and Queen Elizabeth's Coronation, 11-13 May 1937. President of the proceedings was Gomer S. Morgan with David Lukey, the school attendance officer (whipper-in) as organizer. Children were allowed tea at the church hall and the over sixty-fives enjoyed a performance of 'The Feast of Hans' following lunch. At 10 p.m. the bonfire was lit and on the following day the town band performed while a series of sporting events were held.

Filming *Proud Valley* on the Bull Ring *c.* 1939. Black American bass singer Paul Robeson filmed scenes of *Proud Valley* (where the miners march to London) in Llantrisant. The famous performer and political activist stayed a night in the town's police station while filming took place.

Llantrisant Home Guard during the Second World War. The Common became home to a unit of American soldiers during the Second World War. Originally they camped on the top of a disused mine-shaft until they were alerted to the possible dangers involved. They were all units of the Seventh Corps commanded by Major General J. Laughton-Collins ('Lightning Joe' Collins). Many of them lost their lives during the landings on Utah Beach on D-Day, but some fought to the Elbe, over the Rhine and at Remagen Bridge.

Llantrisant & Llantwit Fardre Rural District Council (established 1894) pictured on the Bull Ring following a Civic Sunday Service in 1947. Wearing the chains of office is Ivor Jacob, born in Vicarage Cottage on Heol Las. A Freeman and member of the Town Trust, he served as an elected member for the council for fourteen years and was voted chairman in 1947. Prior to his death in 1949, aged fifty-eight, he also served on Mid Glamorgan County Council.

John (Jack) Morris with his mother Catherine 'Ginny' Jane Morris (1870-1948) and a young Allan May outside Willis the butcher's shop opposite the Cross Keys pub. The present building was divided into three with Gladys, Frank and Allan May living in one home, the Morrises in the second and the butcher's shop on the right. Jack worked as a night-watchman in a warehouse on Newport Road, Cardiff, and was murdered there by two burglars on 28 April 1959. He was sixty years old.

A day trip to the seaside organized by Llantrisant Workingmen's Club, starting from the Bull Ring. Typically a convoy of buses took the excited children and their families to Barry or Porthcawl in alternate years. Despite the opening of Llantrisant railway station in the late 1860s, this isolated junction would later cause the widespread growth of a new-found community, to become known as Pontyclun.

Festival of Britain party in Dan Caerlan, June 1951. This special occasion was commemorated in the town by a series of parties in the streets, while celebration concerts and sports events also took place.

A street party outside the Butcher's Arms, June 1952. The happy event was brought to a premature conclusion when news arrived that Trevor Evans of Dan Caerlan had been captured and was believed to have been killed while fighting in Korea. A far greater celebration was held some months later when he was found alive in a prisoner-of-war camp and returned home safely to his family.

A group of Llantrisant residents enjoying a trip to Blackpool *c.* 1960. Some of the happy holidaymakers include Mr and Mrs Ferris, the Francis sisters and residents of the Common Estate and the old town.

Residents of Dan Caerlan on a trip to Blackpool *c.* 1955. From left to right, back row: Richard Raison, Bill Maslin, Charlie Evans, Jordan Jenkins. Third row: Ernest Stallard, Phyllis O'Marley, Winnie Jenkins, Mr Davies, Morgan Watkins, Mrs Gillard, Nellie Davies, Jean Noyce, Spencer Thomas, Richard Williams, Jack Osborne. Second row: Mrs Hurley, Mrs Maslin, Barbara Williams, Mrs Evans, Mariana Hallett, Diane Evans, June Pemberthy. Front row: May Thurlin, Hettie Stallard, Sadie Williams, Nelly Alford.

Llantrisant Carnival held on the rugby ground at Cefn Mabley in 1953. Pictured from left to right are Dinah Holmes, Vi Hurley, Ivy Bushby and Ron Bushby of Dan Caerlan.

Llantrisant Women's Group pictured at their annual Christmas supper at the York Hotel, Bridgend, c. 1950. The housewives met weekly in the Social Hall ('The Hut').

Right: Nesta Little (Llantrisant sub-postmistress) and her assistant Muriel Thomas were commended for their courage in 1970 by thwarting the attempts of an armed raider on the post office. They enjoyed a reception with the managing director of post offices in London who paid tribute to the two ladies for their outstanding bravery. Miss Little's father, James Little, was postmaster from 1902-1943 and she ran the business from 1943-1969. Her brother, Peter Little, succeeded her as postmaster in 1969 but Miss Little continued in the post of sub-postmistress for many more years, assisted by Miss Thomas.

Below: Angry Llantrisant mothers protesting over the number of lorries travelling through the old town, 30 September 1970. The protestors blocked the road because of the volume of traffic using Newbridge Road when travelling to and from the Royal Mint (opened 1968) and nearby Fram Filters. To the left is Terry's Stores, originally Thomas and Evans.

Llantrisant Town Band with conductor B. Rex. During the 1920s the band was formed with players from Beddau, Cross Inn and Tynant, and rehearsed in the Cross Keys before moving to the former jailhouse below the town hall. The bandmaster was John M. Thomas of Tynant, whose three sons, Tom, Cromwell and Harry, all played the cornet. He was succeeded by Oliver Williams, who remained in the post until 1932 when he took over the baton at Buxton Silver Band in Derby.

Llantrisant Town Band c. 1920. Euphonium player Daniel Williams ('Dan the Band') became conductor in the 1930s while John Thomas was elected secretary. The band performed in concerts and fêtes and in the demonstration marches of 1934. It perished during the Second World War and the last performance was at the Armistice Parade in Beddau. Some of the members included: Cornets: Reuben Jewell, Dai Roberts, Jack Pugh, Cyril Blake, Ronnie Pricket, Owen Bowler, Dai Morris, Ifor Williams, Joe Winter and soprano cornet Joe Williams. Tenor horns: Jim Davies, Alf Williams, Johnny Roberts, Dai Davies. Trombone: Evan James. Euphonium: Will Jewell, Cyril Mercer. Baritone: Frank Games, C. Woodward. Basses: Bert Rees, Bill Wilkins, Bill Coles. E flat bass: Arthur Hooper, Trevor West.

Llantrisant Opera Society's performance of *The Magic Key* in 1927, with vicar Simon. Eisteddfodau were held in public houses, organized by the Cymreigyddion Society, which was formed at the Swan Inn in 1771. Their object was to promote Welsh culture and it reached the height of its power by 1845. In 1865 a very successful eisteddfod was held in the market place to raise funds for a reading room and library at Llantrisant.

Llantrisant Male Voice Choir, 1915. The first record of a male choir in Llantrisant was during a concert on 1 March 1898, after a whist drive on St David's Day. Rehearsals were held at the Wesleyan chapel and conducted by Cliff Davies (stationmaster at Llantrisant railway station) from 1898 to 1912. The present choir was reformed in 1909. It was later conducted by Jenkin Thomas of Miskin, accompanied by Mrs A. Lewis.

Llantrisant Male Voice Party.

Presented
by
Llantrisant Male Voice
Party.
to
Signr E. P. Rex, R.F.A.

as a tribute to the Services he
rendered his King and Country in
the Great War, 1914=1918, when
he loyally served in the Cause of
Liberty, Justice and Righteousness,
against the German attempt to
Conquer by Brute Force.

1914   1918

Presentation by Llantrisant Male Voice Party to E.P. Rex as a tribute to his services during the First World War, 1918. In 1917 they went by horse brake to Southerndown to entertain wounded soldiers at the Red Cross Hospital, and in 1919 they unveiled the war memorial at Miskin. In 1923 Luther Jones, the secretary, was appointed conductor and remained in post for fifty-one years until his death. The accompanist for forty-one years was Lottie Williams of The Firs, followed by Luther's wife, Winifred Jones, for twelve years. In 1968 they sang for Elizabeth II and Prince Philip at the opening of the Royal Mint.

Llantrisant Orpheus Glee Society, 1920. From left to right, back row: S. Hayward, Jack Lukey, J.I. Williams, Jack Barkle, William Griffiths (father of church organist Enid Lewis). Middle row: Lemuel 'The Milk' Evans, Evan Llewellyn, Jack Lamerton, H.H. Richards, H. Warburton, William Morgan (Bull Ring Farm). Front row: Tom Dyer (sanitary worker), G. Williams, David Lukey (whipper-in), Gregory Evans RCM (conductor), F. Wareham (secretary) W.Davies, Ivor Pickford.

Llantrisant Male Voice Choir presentation evening to Reg Westcott for dedicated service to the choir. The presentation was held in the Workingmen's Club and Mr Westcott received a fine armchair from the choir's vice-president Glyn Phillips.

Ruth Harwood's dance troop, c. 1947. Mrs Harwood, of Tonypandy, taught ballet classes in the social hall. They performed concerts with song and dance routines in various locations throughout the town. Members included Maureen Davies, Dorothy John, Sheila David, Ruth Harrison, Mary Williams, Lynne Davies and Monica Holloway.

Enid Griffiths, 1932. Born in 1915 to William Griffiths (1887-1972) and Elizabeth Ann Griffiths (1891-1985), her sister was Betty (Green). Miss Griffiths received piano tuition from Danny Francis of Pontyclun and achieved both the Associate of London College of Music and the Licentiate of the London College of Music. She was married in 1948 to Eric Lewis and the couple settled in High Street. For more than sixty years she taught piano lessons to local children and was organist at Llantrisant parish church for fifty dedicated years. In 2000 she received the MBE for her services to the community.

Penelopen Elizabeth Price (1886-1977) dressed as Britannia in 1918. Culturally, Llantrisant blossomed during the early part of the twentieth century, with such organizations as Miss E. Bowen's Gipsy Chorus. Also William Davies (Alwydd Tydfil) lived here and composed the popular Welsh classic, 'O Na Byddain Haf O Hyd' ('Oh That it Were Always Summer').

Jeffrey Hooper 1974. Born in 1959, Jeff, of Dan Caerlan, won the television talent show *New Faces* in May 1974 with the highest recorded scores of the series for his performance of 'For The Good Times'. He gave his first solo stage performance at Llantrisant RFC clubhouse in 1973. He also appeared on *The Golden Shot* and *Stars on Sunday* before signing an EMI contract. Jeff later performed in the Sands Hotel in Las Vegas, learning his technique from Mel Torme and Matt Monro. He spent a decade with the Syd Lawrence Orchestra and became the lead vocalist with the BBC Big Band. A radio broadcaster, he interviewed Tony Bennett, and launched a succession of big band tours (admired by the late Diana, Princess of Wales). He is now a regular performer on the P&O Cruise Liners and in concert halls throughout the country.

A performance of Aladdin by the Llantrisant Parish Church Mothers Union at the church hall, c. 1960. It was produced by Muriel Davies, the wife of vicar Edwin Davies, and the cast included Tom and Betty Hughes, Mary and Gwyneth Dickason, Mary Williams, Gwyneth Siams Cornelius and Enid Lewis, all of whom remained involved with productions at the hall for the next thirty-five years.

The sport of badger-baiting was commonplace in the town. This crowd were pictured outside Graig House around 1922, and includes Fred Osborne, Arthur John, Oliver John, Dai Williams, baby Gwyneth Williams (later Taylor), Charlie Curslick, Dan Davies, Chrislie and Doris Trewortha, Phyllis Courtney and Dai Lukey.

Llantrisant RFC First XV, 1896/97. Dai Lukey was club captain for the 1899-1900 season. During the 1920s Archie Thomas, one of the forwards, went on to play for Pontypridd and played through a Welsh trial despite suffering a couple of broken ribs early on in the game. Billy Jenkins, another gifted player, went on to play scrum-half for Bridgend and Ponty. The club's playing record for the seasons 1931-1936 was a phenomenal seven losses in five years with a three-year ground record.

Llantrisant RFC First XV, 1923/24. From left to right, back row: W. Meredith, I. Westcott, E. Harrison, P. Dooley, W. Harrison, A. Trewartha, W. Evans, E. Jenkins, A. Thomas, T. Rees, P. Rees, P. Causon. Third row: E. Westcott, W. Phillips, C. Regan. Second Row: P. Croft, J. Clay, J. Harrison, L. John, I. Herbert. Front row: W. Wilkins, D. Davies, D. Davies (captain), W. Jenkins, J. Thomas, J. Jeffries.

Llantrisant RFC 1935/36. From left to right, back row: R. Lukey (chairman), W. Roche (secretary 1934-1935), T.C. Williams (treasurer), G. Birch, O. Raison, Cliff O'Neill, R. Hopkins, C. Williams, Jack Phillips, M. Birch., D. Williams (trainer), R. Owen, H. Wyatt (hon. sec. 1935-36). Middle Row: W. Hicks, T. Davies, D. Israel, C. Trewartha (captain), G. Jenkins, D. Morgan, P. Croft. Front Row: J. Francis, T. Wilkins. In 1945 the club was reformed following the end of the Second World War. A door-to-door collection by the members was the source of much needed clothing coupons and these enabled a kit to be provided for the teams and, because of the war effort, a permit was required from the Ministry of Agriculture in order to get a set of posts from the Maelwg Forestry.

Job Davies wearing his Welsh Cap, 1926 (c. 1905-1960). The youngest of twelve children from Penygawsi, he was a collier boy before joining the Glamorgan Police Force where he was stationed in Bridgend and Maesteg and was capped for Wales in 1926. He played rugby for both sides before joining Pontypridd RFC after being stationed in Pwllgwaun during the 1930s, and also played for Cardiff. In 1938 he became a police sergeant in Llantwit Major and was seconded to St Athan where he trained in the Air Force police. He was the first on the scene at the air crash in Llandow. Job was the younger brother of Dai 'Dogs' Davies, the huntsman.

Llantrisant RCT First XV, 1946/47. From left to right, back row: F. Hurley, C. Williams, C. Harrison, W. Hurley, W. Jenkins, C. Hurley, L. Raison, C. Harrison, D. Griffiths, N. Rees, I. Watkins, P. Montague, F. Martin, L. Williams, B. Rees, C. ONeill, C. Doster, W. Hurley, W. Hicks, G. Jenkins. Middle row: N. Doster, D. Williams, G. Bendle, T. Rees, T. Davies (captain), V. Doster, D. Hill, D. Hurley, Charlie Jordan. Front row: H. Hurley, L. Hurley. Inserts: W. Lamerton, D. Griffiths, W. Jacob (missing), I. Evans.

Trevor 'Chippo' Davies wearing his Cilfynydd RFC kit, *c.* 1938. Born in 1917, he was nicknamed after his father who ran the fish and chip shop on the Bull Ring. He first played for Llantrisant in 1933 and continued turning out on the field for the hometown side for the next twenty-five years. In 1937 he joined Pontypridd RFC and was approached by the hugely successful Cilfynydd side in 1938, where he played a season. The Second World War interrupted his sporting career when he served in the Pioneers at Anzio, Italy, and narrowly survived a train crash. He played one more season for Cilfynydd in 1945, but the iron ore worker, who lived in Dan Caerlan, remained faithful to the Llantrisant side where he was club captain twice.

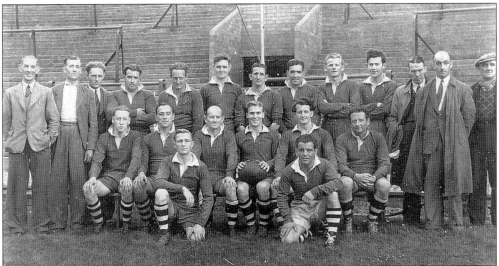

Llantrisant First XV, 1949/50 Mallet Cup finalists. From left to right, back row: D. Williams (assistant trainer), S. Jenkins (chairman), William Williams, H. Jenkins, R. Williams, Dennis Williams, Dennis Hurley, W. Lamerton, Ivor 'Springy' Evans, Watcyn Jacob, Cliff O'Neill (secretary), Viv Phillips (committee), W. Hicks (trainer). Middle row: Ivor Watkins, Eddie Thomas, Trevor Davies, Trevor Rees (captain), Brynley Rees, B. Williams. Front row: Vernon Doster, Charlie Jordan. At the end of the 1940s the club was a member of the Cardiff and District Rugby Union, and was eligible to play in the Mallet Cup competition. Llantrisant reached the final on two occasions but lost to Pentyrch RFC both times. The finals were played on the revered turf of Cardiff Arms Park.

Royston Collins. Born in 1934, he was one of eight children, and attended Llantrisant Junior School and Tonyrefail Grammar School. A gifted outside-half, he played for Llantrisant in 1950 and was later capped as a Welsh Schoolboy during the same year. He was capped a second time in 1953 for Welsh Secondary Schoolboys under-19s and played against England and Scotland. While serving in the RAF he played for Bath, Exeter and Devon and later coached Llantrisant after settling into married life at Ivy Dene on Church Street, while teaching at Pontypridd County School for Boys.

Llantrisant RCT First XV, 1958/59. From left to right, back row: G. Ryley, Dai 'Telly' Thomas, William Thomas, John Harrison, Cyril Harrison, R. Boundford, A. Davis (referee). Middle row: D. Harvey, Idris Doster, Gwyn Ferris (captain), N. Rees, Warren Kendall. Front row: Gwyn Grother, David Jenkins, Len Hurley, Gwyn Doster.

124

Llantrisant First XV, 1971/72. From left to right, back row: D. Drinkwater, Trevor Lloyd, J. Flower, Anthony 'Oxy' Hopkins, A. Lamerton, H. Hughes. Middle row, Gerald Davies, Leighton Williams, Gareth Davies, Wynford Rees, Frank Mercer. Front row: Phillip Newton, Ken Worgan, Roger Lamerton (captain). Mike Wood, D. Williams. R. Lee.

Llantrisant RFC committee members celebrating their acceptance into the WRU in 1983. Pictured from left to right, back row: Tony Kokkinos, David 'Telly' Thomas, Gordon Oliver, Gwilym Treharne, Ray Clarke, Billy Thomas, Mervyn Collins, Ivor Evans, Stuart Fisher, Gordon Jenkins, Allan Watkins, Cliff O'Neill, Watcyn Jacob. Front row: David Jenkins, Nick Woods, Wynford Benyon, Trevor Davies.

Llantrisant Golf Club, 1945. The Town Trust originally allowed golf to be played on the Common in July 1901, but it was from November 1922 until 1927 that the golfers rather controversially played there, calling themselves Llantrisant Freemen's Golf Club. Following massive opposition from the residents, furious at the Trustees for granting permission, the golfers opened their own club and course in Talbot Green. According to Town Trust records, angered Freemen ripped out flags and stole golf balls before throwing them into the Common pond. One group of women allegedly sat on the holes to prevent the golfers from playing.

Gordon Clay (left), pictured with Hugh Squirrel at the final of the Welsh Championships, 1964. Born in Tonyrefail in 1926, before moving to Llantrisant he worked on the golf course in Talbot Green after leaving school. Following active service in the Second World War, he continued his work on the course and progressed to become a talented player. Gordon won the Glamorgan Championship twice, won the championships in Southerndown seven times and represented Wales in the Home International at Porthcawl in 1962.

Llantrisant Women's rugby team, who got together to take part in a carnival on Cefn Mabley field, c. 1952. From left to right, back row: Mrs Gillard, Beryl Rees, Betty Bevan, Katy Evans, Sheila Gillard. Front row: Annie Groves, Muriel Edwards, Blod Ryan, Joyce Doster, Ena Evans.

Butcher's Arms Darts Club, 1946. Sport flourished in Llantrisant for centuries, and there remains the remnants of the ancient Fives Court of the 1790s, built at the rear of the Workingmen's Club on Swan Street, after the local vicar complained the sport was being played too frequently against the churchyard wall. Another existed behind The Pwysty on George Street (formerly the Angel Inn). The town once had a flourishing quoits club and a gymnasium at the National School, plus clubs for tennis, boxing, bull-baiting and cockfighting.

Llantrisant painted by H. Gastineau *c.* 1823.

Acknowledgements

I sincerely hope that readers will derive as much pleasure from this collection of photographs as I have had in compiling it. However, such a volume would not have been possible had it not been for the magnificent response shown by fellow residents of Llantrisant. I would particularly like to thank Gwyn and Moira Williams, Gill and Noel Garnham, Mary and Gwyn Rees, Tony and Mrs Gwyneth Cale, Glynne Holmes, Noel Israel, Enid Lewis, Yvonne and Gordon Miles, Christine and Gerald James, Margaret David and Gwlithyn Bartlett. May I add my gratitude to author J. Barry Davies for allowing me to use exerpts from his book and for proof-reading parts of this publication. Information was also taken from the three editions of *The History of Llantrisant*, written by Sem Phillips (1866), Taliesin Morgan (1898) and Dillwyn Lewis (1982). Thanks also to Pat and Henry Alexander, John Allen, Doris Barwick, Ruth Bowen, Betty and Fred Bryant, George Bryant, Lynda Bryant, Edwin Cale, Gordon Clay, John Clay, Mervyn Collins, Royston Collins, Keith Davies, Malcolm Davies, Trevor Davies, Gwyneth and Mary Dickason, Norman and Carlene Doster, Ena Evans, Ivor Evans, Julie Evans, Nicola and Glenn Evans, Trevor and Diane Evans, Andrew Giles, Glamorgan Records Office, David Griffiths, Mari Griffiths, Tom Griffiths, Brian and Anne Groves, Valerie Harman, Valerie Harris, Brenda Harry, Sue Harvey, Helen Hayward, Viv Holloway, Sue Hughes, Ted Hughes, Watcyn Jacob, Gillian Jenkins, Brenda and Edwyn John, Dorothy John, David John, Edith John, Margaret John, Dr Michael Jones, John Kelland, Dorothy Kokkinos, Dr Faenor Lewis, Edna Little, Llantrisant Library, Llantrisant Male Choir, Llantrisant Rugby Football Club, Llantrisant Town Trust, Llantrisant Workingmen's Club, Maesybryn Primary School, Jimmy Martin, Graham Mellor, Marion Morgan, Bryan Morse, National Library of Wales, Guy Oliver, David Owen, Revd Viv Parkinson, Clive Pegg, *Pontypridd & Llantrisant Observer*, Florence Price, Howard Raison, Glyn Rees, Bronwen Roberts, Margaret Smallman, South Wales Police Authority, Dudley Stephens, Del and Dolph Tate, Gwyneth and Bill Taylor, Howard Thomas, Trefor Thomas, Ismay Thurling, Barbara Walby, Terrance Ward, Brian Westcott, *Western Mail & Echo*, Alf Williams, Glynne Williams, Haydn Williams, Ifor Williams, Mary Williams, Richard Williams.